ARMADA!

ARMADA!

The Planning, the Battle and After

❖

Robert Milne-Tyte

WORDSWORTH EDITIONS

In memory of my sister
Jean Kitson

First published in Great Britain 1988
by Robert Hale Limited, London.

Copyright © 1988 Robert Milne-Tyte
All rights reserved

This edition published 1998
by Wordsworth Editions Limited
Cumberland House, Crib Street, Ware,
Hertfordshire SG12 9ET

ISBN 1 85326 688 4

© Wordsworth Editions Limited 1998

Wordsworth® is a registered trade mark of
Wordsworth Editions Limited

Printed and bound in Great Britain
by Mackays of Chatham PLC, Chatham, Kent.

CONTENTS

List of Maps   6

The Invincible Armada   9
Background to Conflict   13
Interlude at Corunna   18
The English Navy   25
Invasion Imminent   30
The Waiting Game   37
End of an Interlude   44
The Beacons Burn   53
The Battle of Portland Bill   61
Commanders' Concerns   70
The Isle of Wight Battle   75
Anchorage at Calais   81
The Deadly Fireships   88
The Last Conflict   93
'The Most Fearful Day in the World'   100
The Rumour War   106
Tilbury – 'This Place Breedeth Courage'   112
'In Such High Latitudes'   119
A Queen's Reward   126
Disaster in Ireland   132
Prisoners and Fugitives   145
End of a Flawed Enterprise   150

Bibliography   156
Index   158

LIST OF MAPS

The Armada sets Sail for England   8

The Fighting Begins   54

The End of the Armada   120

Armada!

Vanguard of Armada waits off Scillies,
sighted by Capt. Fleming
who raises alarm at Plymouth

SCILLY ISLES

CHERBOURG

Armada struck by Storm

BREST

Struck by Storm, forced
into Corunna Harbour
Armada resumes voyage after
one month stay at Corunna

BAY OF BISCAY

CORUNNA

OPORTO

Armada sets sail end of May,
driven 100 miles south by adverse winds

LISBON
C. ESPICHEL

The Armada
sets sail for
England

0   50   100 mls

1   The Invincible Armada

For almost a year Miguel de Cervantes had ridden the roads of southern Spain requisitioning supplies for the Spanish Armada, but now, with the spring of 1588 shading into summer, his task was at an end – that great fleet was starting to work out of the port of Lisbon, ready to embark upon its holy mission against the heretics of England.

News of the Armada's departure must have stirred in Cervantes' mind the memory of another powerful Spanish fleet, one in which he himself had sailed almost twenty years earlier, when the might of the Turkish navy had been vanquished at the battle of Lepanto. He still bore scars from that conflict, and, at the age of forty-one, he continued to carry too the burden of poverty which had been with him most of his life, for with *Don Quixote* yet to be written, his impoverished obscurity was only equalled by his irrepressible ambition.

But as a requisitioning officer he had served the King of Spain well, 4,000 arrobas of olive oil and 3,000 bushels of grain collected in torrid Ecija, the frying pan of Andalucia, 5,000 bushels of grain in the Cordovan towns of La Rambla and Castro de Rio. All that at a time of bad harvests and with the previous year's requsitions still not paid for – noble service indeed.

Unfortunately for Cervantes, the grain owners had included a number of influential churchmen, and thus, regardless of the royal warrant which he bore, they sought revenge for his zealous effrontery. He was excommunicated, twice, first by the vicar-general of Seville for his assault on the ecclesiastical granaries of Ecija, and a second time by the vicar-general of Cordoba for his similar offence in that region.

Whatever the cost to Cervantes' soul of that double excommunication, he would at least have had the earthly satisfaction of a job well done, King Philip's great enterprise had

been inched forward, 'the invincible Armada' as all Spain had
come to know it, the mightiest fleet ever assembled anywhere,
was just that little more prepared. Soon it would sweep the seas
around England clear of opposition, the heretical Queen
Elizabeth would be deposed, and the true Catholic faith restored
to that benighted land.

That, at least, was the popular expectation as the Armada
worked its way down the Tagus in the late May of 1588. Two
whole days it took for the fleet to assemble at sea, the sixty-five
high-castled, flag-bedecked galleons among its number giving
the entire assemblage the appearance of some floating citadel.
There gathered the royal squadron of Portugal, the squadron of
Castile, the squadron of Andalucia, of Biscay, Guipuzcoa, the
ill-fated Levantine squadron, more than 130 ships in all, and
30,000 men.

Beating up from Cadiz, the Hamburg-bound cargo ship
captained by Hans Limburger first sighted the forest of distant
sail somewhere about Cape Espichel, and although Spanish
preparations had been the talk of Europe for many months, the
vastness of the Armada none the less amazed the crew of the
German ship. For one complete day Captain Limburger's vessel
hauled past a seemingly endless procession of ships, towering
galleons, squat, many-oared galleys, galleasses, larger than the
galleys with fewer oars and more sail, cumbersome *urcas*, the
cargo carriers, swift *pataches* and *zabras*, the eyes of the fleet.
Such a spectacle of power and grandeur had never before been
witnessed at sea at any time or in any place in the world.

A week or so afterwards, in the approaches to the Channel, a
patrolling English warship picked up the Hamburg-bound vessel
and shepherded it into Plymouth, where Captain Limburger was
civilly entertained while the authorities questioned him. And
well he deserved to be entertained, for from him came the first
precise information that the English had been able to glean
about the Spanish fleet's movements. Now, after months of
rumour and uncertainty, it was positively established – the
Armada was on its way.

'His mother fell in labour with him upon the fright of the
invasion of the Spaniards.' Thus John Aubrey wrote concerning
the birth in 1588 of his eminent friend, the philosopher, Thomas
Hobbes. The alarm felt by Hobbes's mother was justified

enough, fuelled as it was by the dire, doom-laden prophecies which flew around England at that time. The Spanish were coming, it was cried abroad, with shiploads of halters to hang all Englishmen, with scourges to whip the women, with 4,000 wet nurses to suckle babies orphaned by the conflict. Children between seven and twelve would be branded in the face, declared one rumour; the entire population between seven and seventy was to be exterminated, said another.

It was the dread engendered in Mrs Hobbes by such reports to which, in later years, her famous son attributed 'his extreme timorousness', according to Aubrey.

Yet had the English been aware of the profound reservations held by the King of Spain's principal commanders as they helped shape his great enterprise, could they have known the fatal imperfections in both the planning and equipping of the project, then many an anxious hour might have been avoided.

On the face of things, the venture was relatively straightforward; the Spanish fleet was to force its way up the Channel for a rendezvous with the Duke of Parma, Spain's most illustrious general, whose polyglot army, battle-hardened by years of service in the Spanish Netherlands, would be waiting at ports along the coast of Flanders. The Armada would then shepherd Parma's shoal of landing craft to invasion sites in the Thames estuary, from where, accompanied by troops from the fleet itself, his men would march upon London.

When put to the test, however, such apparently simple designs frequently fall apart as unforeseen mischance intrudes; sod's law rules, in other words, and King Philip's enterprise was fated to become a classic victim of that law.

Mischance apart, what Thomas Hobbes's mother could not know as her acute anxiety brought on the pangs of childbirth was that one simple, fundamental flaw above all others would doom the project to confusion and disaster – the total lack of effective communication between the sea and land forces involved.

Here was an operation quite as complicated in its time as the Allied invasion of France in 1944, and yet, whereas the latter was the product of months of detailed first-hand cooperation between the numerous key officers, the Armada's commander, the Duke of Medina Sidonia, never once came face-to-face with the land-based Duke of Parma. In fact, the exchange of information between them even by messenger, was almost non-existent until it was too late to matter.

Added to that, the Spaniards sailed into the Channel in that August week of 1588 to discover that the art of naval warfare had been advanced by the English almost as radically as when, over three centuries later on the battlefield, tanks first confronted cavalry.

Suddenly the hitherto successful tactics of the Spanish navy were obsolete, no longer could its galleons triumph, as they had done at Lepanto and elsewhere, by grappling with enemy vessels and pouring troups aboard. The agile ships and long-range guns with which the English had equipped themselves, never, in nine days of fighting, allowed the Spaniards to get near enough to grapple.

And in scraping together his massive fleet, the Spanish King had made scant allowance for the perversity of the weather around England's coasts, or for the violence of northern seas. When, in that wretched summer of 1588 the Armada enterprise was crumbling in storm-racked waters, numerous ships were lost because, built for the calmer Mediterranean, their seams opened under the relentless battering they received.

With the benefit of 400 years of hindsight it can be seen that the Spanish Armada was the nearest thing ever to a pre-ordained disaster, because even if one sets aside the factors which principally frustrated it – the skill and tenacity of the English navy and the unusually adverse weather – the task of transporting thousands of troops across the Channel in shallow barges designed for Flanders waterways and putting them safely ashore on Kent beaches would have demanded such a complex combination of wind, weather and tides as to have occurred relatively rarely. Had such a feat been achieved it would have required a considerable slice of luck even with minimal resistance from the defending English militia. And luck was a severely restricted commodity in the Armada.

The common people of Elizabethan England were not to know that, however, as far as they were concerned it was a moment of extreme peril. Mrs Hobbes and thousands like her had reason to be fearful. The most powerful nation in the world had assembled the largest fleet ever to put to sea with the avowed purpose of rooting out English Protestantism.

In the event, after days of tension, the Armada crisis simply evaporated, the Spanish fleet ultimately losing more ships to wind, weather and Irish rocks than to English guns. So it never developed, like Waterloo, into 'the nearest run thing you ever saw in your life.' And yet it still ranks as one of the most significant episodes in the history of England, a potential watershed in precisely the manner of Waterloo or the Battle of Britain.

To the Spanish, it was God's work they were about, yet bewilderingly, the mission was a costly failure. Maybe, on that occasion, at least, God was an Englishman.

2   *Background to Conflict*

By the summer of 1588 a state of undeclared war had existed for some four years between England and Spain, a pin-prick kind of war, waged partly on land, partly at sea. The slow spread of Protestantism in Europe was a serious threat to the interests of Catholic Spain, nowhere more so than in the Spanish Netherlands, where revolt smouldered constantly. The Duke of Parma, forty-two years old in the Armada year, son of the King of Spain's half-sister, had commanded the Spanish forces there since 1578, and seemed to have struck a decisive blow when, six years later, his agents successfully engineered the assassination of his principal adversary, the Prince of Orange.

At that point, however, the English intervened, supplying troops and money to bolster the faltering Dutch. In 1587, with the war dragging on, Spanish passions were further inflamed by the execution of Mary, Queen of Scots, on whom rested their hopes as the Catholic alternative to heretical Elizabeth on the throne of England.

Beyond these events, though, lay the exasperation and damaged pride caused to King Philip by the buccaneering exploits of English seamen, most notably Sir Francis Drake.

By the time of the Armada, such was Drake's renown that his portrait was in demand throughout Europe, the portrait of a man described thus by one Spaniard who had encountered him, 'of medium stature, blond, rather heavy than slender, merry, careful.'

The exploits of this 'merry, careful' marauder had made him hated, feared, respected wherever Spanish was spoken, for no Spaniard, at home or in the wide empire, could feel entirely impervious to the threat he posed. Certainly no Spanish seaman could sleep easy in his hammock when Drake was afloat, for since that time in 1573 when he and his crew had captured a vast haul of gold and silver from a Spanish mule-train in the Panama isthmus, each succeeding exploit had outdone the previous one. In 1580 he had circled the entire globe in his doughty ship, the *Golden Hind*, returning to Plymouth with eastern treasure, jewels, silks, spices, gold, sufficient to yield for his backers profits of almost 5,000 per cent.

Subsequently he and his squadron had roamed at will along the coast of Spain, across the Atlantic, and up and down the Spanish Main, capturing and burning colonial settlements, plundering stores, harrying the treasure fleets on their voyages from South America. In 1586, not a single piece of silver reached Spain from the mines of Mexico and Peru, to the near ruin of some of the nation's greatest trading houses and the intense alarm of King Philip's bankers.

Fortunately for England, Spain's response to these provocations was a slow-building affair. But if the Spanish needed time to prepare their offensive, England's need of time was even more acute since, defensively, she was as unready when the Armada threat first loomed as when the clouds of conflict with Nazi Germany gathered in the 1930s.

'Such as have followed the wars are despised of every man until a very pinch of need doth come,' was the bitter comment of one English professional soldier of that age, and, indeed, his words were all too true.

By comparison with the rest of Europe, and with Spain's experienced professional troops in particular, the English were the rankest amateurs in the art of soldiering, without a regular army and with little more than a skeletal and ill-trained militia when the crisis developed in the early 1580s.

And despite some improvements by 1588, had the Armada

succeeded in putting troops ashore, the English must have been desperately hard-pressed to contain them.

The moderately effective coastal defences which Elizabeth inherited on ascending the throne had been allowed to deteriorate in the ensuing two and more decades of peaceful prosperity, and the militia had grown slack.

The navy, too, was in little better shape at the beginning of the 1580s, poorly administered and with most of its ships in poor condition. If Francis Drake stands as the most daring, most resolute mariner of Elizabethan England, then to his fellow-Devonian, John Hawkins, must go the credit for rescuing the navy from its long decline and for fashioning the new breed of warships which thwarted the might of the Armada.

But the measures needed to check decay on land and sea were hideously expensive, the expense made harder to bear by the fact that it was a time of deep economic depression, with England's cloth trade seriously damaged by war.

And the longer Spain delayed the launching of its Armada, the greater the cost to England, with each day bringing new demands on the state coffers, themselves almost depleted. So that eventually Lord Burghley, Queen Elizabeth's principal minister, was moved to exclaim in exasperation, 'A man could wish if peace cannot be had that the enemy would no longer delay, but prove, as I trust, his evil fortune.'

The fact was that for months, Lord Burghley had been the target of a mounting chorus of complaint, from city and shire alike, concerning the 'insupportable charges' with which they were being burdened.

'I assure you,' he wrote to Sir Francis Walsingham, the queen's secretary, 'that I know that whole towns pay as much as four subsidies; so it will be very unreasonable to demand new subsidies.'

If the poor were not included in these demands, he added, the matter would be of less concern because the rich could probably afford to pay more, but as it was, 'I see a general murmer of people, and malcontented people will increase, to the comfort of the enemy.'

The sort of unwelcome demand from the Crown which Englishmen were finding themselves saddled with at this time was that which arrived at Darley Hall, the Derbyshire home of Roger Columbell Esquire. After setting out the dangers threatened by Spain, and the cost of meeting them, the missive continued, '– we have, therefore, thought it expedient, having always our good and loving subjects most ready upon such like occasions to furnish us by way of a loan (which we have and mind always to repay) to have recourse to them in like manner at this present – wherefore we require you to pay to our use the sum of five-and-twenty pounds.'

This peremptory request, today's equivalent of more than £2,000, was met by Columbell some weeks before the Armada appeared, he being all too aware, one imagines, that in spite of the Crown's promise to repay, he was unlikely ever to see his money again.

The owner of Darley Hall had shown himself more patriotic, or perhaps more wary of the State's long arm, than the gentry of the nearby county of Northamptonshire, because even as the Armada sailed up the Channel, the lord lieutenant there, Sir Christopher Hatton, was having to nag away at his deputy lieutenants, urging them 'to use all necessary persuasions' to ensure the Northamptonshire tax assessments were met.

Such reluctance in the face of Spain's growing threat was by no means uncommon, with many a citizen suspicious that, in the usual way of things, the special assessments levied to meet the emergency would eventually become permanent taxes.

In the light of such a situation it was hardly surprising that Sir Francis Walsingham should cry with a note of anguish in his voice, 'I am sorry to see so great a danger hanging over this realm so slightly regarded and so carelessly provided for. Would to God the enemy were no more careful to assail than we to defend.'

After the long years of peace during Elizabeth's reign, the task of bringing the nation's defences to an adequate state of readiness was an arduous and frustrating one for the authorities. Quite apart from the general shortage of money, there seemed, as Walsingham could see, a surprising inability, or unwillingness, in many parts of England to accept that a Spanish invasion was a genuine possibility, a fact illustrated just a few months before the arrival of the Armada by the failure of no fewer than fourteen counties to supply the government with any details whatsoever of their annual militia musters for 1587. In Dorset, one of the counties most vulnerable to invasion, the lord lieutenant dared not submit a muster certificate to London because armour supposed to have been supplied to the militia three years earlier had still not been purchased.

Although by the summer of 1588, the best of the militia had been formed into mobile trained bands, able to move relatively rapidly to points of danger, the rehabilitation of the land forces was a slow business, hampered by social jealousies and regional friction. It was difficult, for instance, to create an efficient chain of command when officers were loath to accept orders from more senior officers of equal or lower social standing. And since the size of a unit often depended on the status of its commander rather than his military ability, it was as well such units were never put to the test of combat.

It was similarly difficult to forge unified militia forces when from every side came claims for special treatment based on antique practice. Liverpool, for example, successfully fought to muster and train men independently of the rest of Lancashire, and elsewhere, London declared itself a county in its own right, while towns such as Abingdon, Chichester, Southampton and Winchester all quoted ancient rights as reasons for not cooperating with the rest of their counties. Meanwhile, the universities of Oxford and Cambridge refused to have anything at all to do with mustering, which led the rest of the inhabitants of those two cities to claim similar exemptions.

By this time a few of the more concerned town councils were beginning to purchase arms and armour of their own (Bath and Hereford had two of the earliest public armouries) but the chief suppliers of funds and equipment continued to be the three traditional sources, the aristocracy, the gentry and the church.

Some of the bishops had enough military hardware under their control to equip a small regiment, a fact which led many a lord lieutenant to look enviously at the church's resources. Indeed, as invasion fever began to mount in the early months of 1588, Archbishop Whitgift of Canterbury found it expedient to indicate to the Bishop of London that whereas the church had rightly stood aloof from the militia in the past, at such a time of national emergency, generous voluntary supplies of arms were desirable – a move clearly designed to divert criticism of ecclesiastical wealth.

Not that much of the church's money, or that of the aristocracy, would ever filter down through the ranks of the militiamen. They themselves, learning to grapple with the pike and the vagaries of the new-fangled harquebus and musket – and probably lamenting the decline of the bow and arrow – would be lucky to be paid more than eight pence a day, less than three pounds at today's prices. The priests who accompanied them would get five times as much.

And by some incredibly perverse process of logic, the cost of powder with which they charged their weapons was deducted from the pay of troops when they were actually in combat, so the harder they fought the poorer they were liable to become. Since, on their eight pence a day, they would also have been levied in time of war for contributions to the pay of priest, surgeon, clerk and muster-master, it was hardly surprising that soldiering in Elizabeth's England was seldom a trade to be followed 'until a very pinch of need doth come.'

3　*Interlude at Corunna*

Towards the end of June, some four weeks after the Armada had left the Tagus, the King of Spain received from its commander the following disturbing assessment: 'I am bound to confess that I see very few, or hardly any, of those on the Armada with any knowledge of, or ability to perform the duties entrusted to them. I have tested and watched this point very carefully, and your Majesty may believe me when I assure you we are very weak.'

That was part of a message despatched by the Duke of Medina Sidonia from the northern Spanish port of Corunna, where, after nearly three weeks of painfully slow sailing from its point of assembly, the main body of the Spanish fleet had sought shelter when struck by the first of the many storms it was destined to encounter.

Now, as the English navy, alerted by Captain Limburger's report, scoured the approaches to the Channel and puzzled over the non-appearance of the Spaniards, they themselves waited at Corunna for the thirty or forty vessels which, having failed to reach the safety of the harbour on the night of the storm, were beginning to drop into ports all along the northern coast of Spain, battered and leaky in many instances, but still afloat.

To Medina Sidonia, this unanticipated interlude was a time for candour, the first miserable phase of the voyage had demonstrated all too clearly the scale of the problems facing the Armada, it was therefore imperative for King Philip to be given the cold facts, since he alone would decide whether the enterprise was to continue.

There had been trouble from the moment the fleet left the Tagus, with rotting food and foul water causing widespread sickness, and adverse winds hampering progress. By English standards, by the new standards of warfare which the Spanish were about to experience, there was hardly a single decent sailing vessel in the entire Armada, the galleons, with their cumbersome fighting castles fore and aft, were slow and difficult enough to handle, but far worse were the *urcas*, the cargo carriers. There were a couple of dozen of these, squat, deep-bellied craft chartered from their Baltic owners and designed for work around the coasts of Europe rather than the open sea. Their sailing qualities were pathetic, so that after more than a week afloat, the north-bound fleet found that it was actually about a hundred miles south of the point from which it had started.

Eventually the northerly winds relented, however, and on a fair southwester the Armada could at last progress in its intended direction; but it was an arduous passage, with more men falling sick each day, and the inadequacies of the enterprise increasingly apparent to Medina Sidonia.

At the time he dictated his discouraging message to King Philip his first thought had been to dissuade the monarch from demanding that the fleet sail on, regardless of the missing ships and their 6,000 men, but it seems clear that those early weeks at sea had seriously undermined his belief in the entire project.

Even when united with the Duke of Parma's army, his letter continued, the Spaniards would still be too weak, and heaven help the Armada if the two forces actually failed to unite because there was not the least chance of finding reinforcements elsewhere.

When Spain had annexed Portugal (in 1580) Medina Sidonia reminded the king, 'I recall the great force your Majesty collected for the conquest – although that country had boundaries with our own and many of its people were in your favour. Well, sir, how do you think we can attack so great a country as England with such a force as ours is now?

'I have earnestly commended this matter to God,' the letter continued, 'and feel bound to put it before your Majesty, so that you may choose the best course for your service while the Armada is refitting here. This opportunity might be taken, and the difficulties avoided, by making honourable terms with the enemy.'

When set alongside the gloomy reports King Philip had been receiving for some time from the Duke of Parma in Flanders, that despatch from Medina Sidonia must have induced any man of less than blind religious faith to cut his losses and abandon the entire undertaking.

Because Parma's reservations were obviously considerable, and growing more so, month by month. In March he had reported, 'Matters generally are proceeding, with the exception of the lamentable and astonishing mortality among the troops. Out of the 28,000 or 30,000 I had hoped to ship, in truth I cannot now find more than 17,000.'

The king had already decreed that Parma's forces would be stiffened for the invasion of England by troops carried by the Spanish fleet, but this does little to diminish his pessimism. 'Even if the Armada supplies me with 6,000 Spaniards as agreed – and they are the sinew of the operation – I shall still have too few troops as the men here are dwindling daily,' he dolefully asserts.

Two weeks later, King Philip is subjected to another discouraging message from Parma. 'Since God has been pleased to defer for so long the sailing of the Armada from Lisbon,' he begins, with perhaps a hint of scepticism, 'we are bound to conclude that it is for His greater glory, and the more perfect success of the business, since the object is so exclusively for the promotion of His holy cause.'

But, Parma continues, the slow nature of the Spanish preparations has given the English ample warning, 'so that it is manifest that the enterprise, which at one time was so easy and so safe, can now only be carried out with infinitely greater difficulty and at a much larger expenditure of blood and trouble.'

This slow build-up of the Armada was due largely to the sheer size and complexity of the operation, but certainly another major handicap had been the sudden death, in February 1588, of the original commander, Spain's most experienced admiral, the Marquis of Santa Cruz.

He died at the age of sixty-two, worn out, it was said, with the care and labour of shaping King Philip's mighty enterprise, and the constant carping of the king himself.

In his place was appointed the Duke of Medina Sidonia, almost twenty-five years younger, the foremost grandee of Spain, brave, resolute, tenacious, but in matters of the sea, a noble novice.

The duke's formal response to the news that he had been selected to replace Santa Cruz could hardly have inspired the Spanish king, even if a degree of self-deprecation was common in such situations.

In seeking to decline the appointment, in a letter to King Philip's secretary, Medina Sidonia had at the outset touched on about as fundamental an objection as could be imagined. '– I have not the health for the sea,' he complained, 'for I know from the small experience I have had afloat that I soon become seasick.'

But his reservations ranged well beyond that acutely personal matter. For one thing, his estate in Andalucia was nearly one million ducats in debt, so that not a single *real* would be available for the expedition (in the end the Armada cost him many thousands more).

'Apart from this, neither my conscience nor my duty will allow me to take this service upon me,' he protested. 'The force is so great and the undertaking so important, that it would not be right for a person like myself, possessing no experience of seafare or war, to take charge of it.'

He had not the slightest knowledge of the Armada's composition, the duke continued, nor the persons taking part in it, the objects in view, the intelligence from England, or the arrangements which Santa Cruz had been making for months past.

'So, sir, you will see that my reasons for declining are so strong and convincing in his Majesty's own interests that I cannot attempt a task of which I have no doubt I should give a bad account,' he pleaded. 'I should be travelling in the dark and should have to be guided by the opinions of others, of whose good or bad qualities I know nothing, and which of them might seek to deceive or ruin me.'

Presumably King Philip had anticipated some such response because he remained firmly resolved, 'But it is I who must judge of your capabilities and parts, and I am fully satisfied with these,' he informed the duke.

The Venetian ambassador to Spain was another who valued Medina Sidonia at a higher price than he appeared to value himself. 'This nobleman,' he reported, 'has excellent qualities and is generally beloved. He is not only prudent and brave, but of a nature of extreme goodness and benignity. He will be followed by many nobles and by all of Andalucia.'

Plucked reluctantly from the ordered calm of his estate near Cadiz, the duke had arrived in Lisbon soon after the death of the Marquis of Santa Cruz to find chaos reigning. With the Armada project losing momentum during the old marquis's last days, desertions had multiplied alarmingly, and among those who remained, many had not been paid for months, while others were without arms or even adequate clothing. Aboard ship the situation was just as disturbing, some vessels being almost without food, some laden too deeply for safety, others virtually unballasted. Certain ships had too many guns, others virtually none; some had plenty of guns but no ammunition, others ammunition but no guns.

But if the Armada commander knew little of seamanship or war, he knew a good deal about the fitting-out of ships. For almost a decade he had been charged with that task as Captain-General of Andalucia, so that by the time he was despatched to Lisbon he was regarded as an expert in all branches of staff work. The fact that the fleet was waiting to sail only a few weeks after he had inherited Santa Cruz's chaos showed that, no matter what the duke's abilities at sea, King Philip had chosen a competent organizer.

All the same, he must have been thankful that his predecessor's original plans had been scaled down, because those plans called for a gigantic force of more than 550 ships and some 90,000 men.

The victualling, alone, of such a massive fleet would have

presented horrifying problems, since even with a force less than one-third that size, the Armada's supply problems were never satisfactorily resolved.

The rotting food and stinking water which many ships found they were carrying on leaving Lisbon resulted mainly from the problem of storage over relatively long periods before the fleet sailed. Even so, several of the principal contractors were said to have been imprisoned as a result.

Whatever the cause, widespread sickness followed, so the storm which forced the Armada into Corunna was a kind of blessing since it enabled fresh food and water to be found, and the sick to recover. On the other hand, had the fleet not been forced to seek shelter, had it maintained its course to England, then the spread of illness and shortage of victuals might well have caused the venture to be aborted long before the Channel was reached, in which case, many a life would have been saved.

As he waited at Corunna for his scattered ships to reassemble, the Duke of Medina Sidonia was anxiously digesting one concern above all others, the problem of water supplies.

Part of the trouble has long been attributed, probably with accuracy, to Sir Francis Drake, because the previous summer, Drake had, in his own words, 'singed the King of Spain's beard' in a series of raids along the coasts of Spain and Portugal. Among the many cargoes seized from Spanish supply ships heading towards the Armada's assembly port of Lisbon was reputed to have been a consignment of barrel staves, which were duly burned. Those staves should have provided new water casks for the Spaniards, and in their absence, old and faulty casks had been pressed into service.

The water problem was amplified by the fact that not only had some 30,000 men to be supplied, but also the numerous cavalry horses and pack animals who sailed with the Armada; they required large quantities daily.

'It is true we carry six months' supply,' the duke wrote to the Duke of Parma, 'but I do not see where we can obtain any more, and it will be advisable for your Excellency at once to consider how we may be aided in this respect, even if it be necessary to transport water in boats from Dunkirk, unless your Excellency knows of any port where both shelter and water may be obtained, which would be a very great point gained.'

As with most of Medina Sidonia's communications to Parma,

there was no response, and survivors of the Armada were to suffer agonies of thirst as they struggled back to home ports.

Meantime, with more and more of the missing ships making their way to Corunna, their commander awaited the King of Spain's decision on whether the project was to proceed. He had voiced his own strong reservations, but he probably realized that the likelihood of it being abandoned was extremely remote.

An array of imperatives demanded that it proceed, principal among them being the religious significance of the venture, but there was also the cold economic fact that success would add to the beleaguered coffers of the Spanish crown the gift of one million gold ducats from the Pope, the wily, cynical Sixtus the Fifth.

Already King Philip had tried, through his ambassador at the Vatican, to wheedle an advance payment from Sixtus, but the old man had proved adamant – the money would only be forthcoming once Spanish troops had set foot on English soil.

'We might as well cry for the moon,' the ambassador lamented in a despatch to Philip, 'as to ask for it before. I am trembling that he may give me many a bitter pill, even before I can get it, seeing how he seems to love this money.'

Indeed, Pope Sixtus had become angry about lack of news on the Armada, no one had thought to inform him of its sailing, and thus the Spanish ambassador was forced to invent the story that a consignment of mail had been lost while on its way through France.

As to King Philip's decision, Medina Sidonia received that in a despatch dated 5 July. The monarch, attentive as usual to every detail, wanted to know at the outset about the ships missing after the storm – could the foreign crews on board a number of them have played a trick on the rest of the fleet, he demanded suspiciously?

In fact, most of the absentees had returned by the date of the despatch, so Medina Sidonia had lost his main reason for not proceeding. And it was, indeed, the king's decision that he should proceed.

He was ordered to use his reserve funds to purchase new supplies, and then to sail. But, apparently referring to some sharp practice to which Medina Sidonia had been subjected at Lisbon, the king had added as a footnote in his own handwriting, 'But you must take great care that the stores are

really preserved, and not allow yourself to be deceived as you
were before.'

In the light of the way in which he had forged order out of
chaos after inheriting Santa Cruz's mantle some five months
earlier, that admonition must have rankled with the Armada's
commander.

4 *The English Navy*

In the early weeks of 1588, the Duke of Parma had proposed
negotiations to Queen Elizabeth, and she, ever anxious to reduce
the drain on State funds, had been pleased to accept. In reality, the
Spanish had not the slightest intention of abandoning the
Armada project, but owing to its slow preparation it was expedient to buy time, to lull the English into thinking that conflict could
be avoided, and so slow down their own plans.

Thus a delegation, led by Sir James Croft, was despatched to
Parma's headquarters in Flanders. But if the talks beguiled the
queen into believing peace might be possible, or that she could
flatter the duke into abandoning his allegiance to Spain and
creating himself ruler of the territory he held in Europe, such
optimism was shared by few others, least of all the seamen who
would confront the Spaniards if, and when, they came.

For despite the negotiations, reports on the Armada
preparations continued to flood in, so that Francis Drake was
moved to warn Elizabeth bluntly, 'The promise of peace from
the Prince of Parma and these mighty preparations in Spain
agree not well together.'

None the less, Sir James Croft's mission was, in the queen's
view, an excellent opportunity to save money, and so, to the
angry despair of its commanders, the navy was ordered to
discharge half its crews.

If the Spaniards suddenly appeared, warned the disgruntled

commander-in-chief, Lord Howard of Effingham, it would take time to remuster those crews, and there might not be time. Furthermore, he pointed out to the queen's secretary, Sir Francis Walsingham, with the fleet so reduced, Spain could land troops in Scotland and threaten England from there, 'for they know we are like bears tied to stakes, and they may come as dogs to offend us, and we cannot go to hurt them.'

In fact, with the death of the Marquis of Santa Cruz putting a brake on Spanish preparations, the ever-audacious Francis Drake was soon proposing a new policy to the Privy Council, a bold and original plan based on the oft-proved maxim that offence is the best form of defence. What he called for was a pre-emptive strike against the Armada, '– with fifty sail of shipping,' he urged, 'we shall do more good upon their own coast than a great many more will do here at home.'

Drake was no particular favourite of Queen Elizabeth, in her view his exploits often caused more friction with Spain than they were worth, but after a visit to Court in early May, he succeeded in getting his plan accepted.

One month later, the fleet set course for Spain under the command of Lord Howard, but bad weather soon forced it back into Plymouth Sound, where to the chagrin of its senior officers, an order was received, revoking the mission.

To Elizabeth and her cautious councillors, anxious reflection had brought the conclusion that it was too risky an undertaking after all. Lord Howard was informed of the Council's chief fear, namely that if the English ships succeeded in reaching their intended destination off Vigo Bay, in north-west Spain, there to challenge the Spanish fleet, 'the said fleet may take some other way, whereby they may escape your lordship, as by bending their course westward to the latitude of 50°, and then to shoot over to this realm –.'

It was now the queen's view that in place of such a chance-laden venture, the navy should 'ply up and down in some indifferent place between the coast of Spain and this realm, so that you may be able to answer any attempt that the said fleet shall make either against this realm, Ireland or Scotland ...'

The indignation of the navy at this reversal of strategy was all too apparent in the reply despatched to Sir Francis Walsingham by Lord Admiral Howard.

'Sir,' he declared, after an expression of profound astonishment at the decision, 'for the meaning we had to go on the coast of Spain, it was deeply debated by those I think the world doth judge to be men of the greatest experience that this realm hath; which are these, Sir Francis Drake, Mr Hawkins, Mr Frobisher and Mr Thomas Fenner; and I hope her Majesty will not think we went rashly to work or without a principal and choice care and respect to the safety of the realm.'

Had the plan been adhered to, Howard went on, the Armada would never have put to sea with the threat of English warships at their backs. But now, under the new instructions, the navy was to be hobbled. If the Spanish picked up a westerly wind and steered for either Ireland or Scotland, then even if the English lay as far north as Cape Clear (south-west Ireland) they would never be able to tackle the Spaniards effectively with the wind in the west. And should they station themselves in that northerly position in anticipation of landings in Ireland or Scotland, the Armada might instead hug the coast of France and strike at the Isle of Wight, with the English too distant to intercept.

The Lord Admiral accepts, however, that it is a time of crisis, and since orders are orders, 'I must and will obey.' But he goes on to inform Sir Francis Walsingham, with his annoyance plainly visible, 'I am glad there be such there as are liable to judge what it is fittest for us to do, than we are here; but by my instructions I did think otherwise, but I will put them up in a bag ...'

Lord Howard could perhaps afford to speak his mind more forcefully than some of his colleagues since, like the Armada's commander, he was a product of high breeding, a first cousin, in fact, of Queen Elizabeth's mother, Anne Boleyn.

There were a number of more experienced captains in the English fleet, most notably, Francis Drake, but Drake, son of a hedge-parson, was serving as second-in-command, having accepted the iron convention of that time that high command and high breeding went hand in hand.

By comparison with the Duke of Medina Sidonia, Lord Howard, who was fifty-two, had a wealth of sea experience, having commanded ships of war for almost twenty years, but alongside Drake, his stature diminished considerably and it might not have been surprising had Drake proved difficult to handle, particularly since he had surrendered influence, income and privileges by placing himself under Howard's command.

Happily this does not happen. 'I must not omit to let you know,' the Lord Admiral is able to inform Walsingham, 'how lovingly and kindly Sir Francis Drake beareth himself.' Perhaps he might be given some word of commendation, Howard suggested.

It was as well there was harmony, and it owed much to the emollient Lord Admiral himself. Had he not been able to persuade the highly individualistic senior commanders of the navy to work closely together in that period of mounting tension and frustration, then things could have gone very ill for England when the Armada came.

The core of the navy in 1588 was small, only a couple of dozen warships and a handful of pinnaces, and although this nucleus was reinforced by armed merchantmen and a host of lesser vessels as the Spanish threat grew, the ships of the royal navy were 'the sinew of the operation' in just the way the Duke of Parma predicted those 6,000 crack Spanish troops would be who were to join him from the Armada.

From the time in 1580 when he assumed responsibility for the maintenance of the queen's royal ships, John Hawkins had concentrated on a policy of rebuilding and remodelling. The idea of the warship as little more than a heavily-garrisoned, floating fortress, with towering castles fore and aft, was seen by the English as totally outdated – the development of the long-range gun had signalled the end of that concept. Having, unlike the Spaniards, rejected the long-established idea that naval warfare consisted of grappling and boarding, England's ship designers were free to concentrate on a new generation of vessels, virtually bereft of castles, long, low-built and with improved sails, vessels 'snug to the water', fast and wonderfully nimble.

The potential of the long-range gun had also been recognized by Hawkins and his senior colleagues to a far greater extent than it had by the Spaniards. At the time of the Armada, six out of every ten guns aboard the queen's ships were heavy calibre weapons, able to hurl cannon balls up to 50 lb in weight hundreds of yards. The Spanish vessels carried many fewer big guns, a fact partly accounting, in all probability, for their failure to sink a single English ship during the nine days of fighting.

Although, on land, the militia might still be raw and

unproven, by the standards of the day, the English at sea were masters of gunnery, 'handy, and without fear about their ordinance.' Their skills were further enhanced by the development of shipboard gun mountings on the royal ships, allowing relatively heavy guns to be fired directly through portholes rather than from field guns sited on maindecks, which continued to be the technique employed in other navies.

The role which gunnery was likely to play if the Spanish came had been acknowledged by the creation in 1586 of a register of gunners. No man on that register was allowed to leave England.

But although gunners could be stayed, guns could not, and the Spaniards, years behind in the art of gunmaking, were desperate to get their hands on heavy weapons wherever they could be found. The ease with which they were able to acquire cannon manufactured in England was a subject of bitter complaint by Sir Walter Raleigh, the chief culprits being a group of merchants in the Bristol area. As late as 1587, nine shiploads of war material 'lead, powder, ordnance and muskets' had been despatched from there to Spain.

And Ralph Hogge, the royal gunfounder, was another who was incensed by this trade. He protested to the Privy Council about the way in which some of his rivals were illegally exporting guns. As a result, no fewer than seventy-seven foundry owners were summoned before the Council and warned.

Even so, many a tempting offer was dangled before the gunmakers, and many an unlicensed cannon found its way to Lisbon or Cadiz.

One well-tried method of evading export regulations on big guns was to cast smaller-calibre weapons, which could be sent abroad without restriction, but to make them of such a diameter that the purchaser could later rebore them to take larger shot. Another method was straightforward smuggling, and only a few months before the Armada left Lisbon, Spanish agents in Europe were trying to obtain English guns in that way, with 20,000 crowns as the bait.

But if the queen's navy was well equipped with guns, powder and shot were in extremely short supply. Francis Drake was reprimanded for expending precious powder on training his crews in rapid firing (during the Armada battles the English fired at three times the rate of the Spaniards, on the latter's own admission) and when his squadron received its allocation of powder in the spring of 1588, he complained that it was only one-third of what was needed, and would suffice for no more than one-and-a-half days.

The problem was that most powder supplies had to be imported, owing to the scarcity of the main ingredient, saltpetre; and although a German army captain was persuaded with a large bribe to reveal the secret of producing it artificially, as was done in his own country, the amount produced by the artificial method fell far short of requirements.

The situation had been eased a little a few years before the Armada when large supplies of saltpetre were discovered in Morocco – it had previously come from the east. A deal, kept secret from Spain, was struck with the Shereef, whereby he received English munitions in exchange for his precious commodity.

Even so, at the end of the conflict with the Armada powder supplies in the English fleet were all but exhausted, and pieces of plough-chain were being used as shot.

5   *Invasion Imminent*

While the navy chafed at the restrictions under which it was being placed, and at its supply problems, preparations on land to resist invasion were being pushed on daily. A force of 1,000 veterans of the war in the Spanish Netherlands had been recalled to stiffen the untried militia, and by mid-June, when news of the sailing of the Armada had been gleaned from Captain Limburger, orders were issued for all officers to remain at home on call, and all troops to be ready for action at one hour's notice.

In the five years prior to 1588, two national surveys had been made, the first to check on the state of fortifications, the second to pinpoint the most likely invasion sites; neither made reassuring reading and each had led to the same conclusion, that a lot of money would be needed to put things right.

The report on Dorset, for example, showed that in the previous five years not one penny of Crown funds had been spent on fortifications, while other vulnerable targets such as Portsmouth, Dover and the Isle of Wight were all very poorly defenced.

In the opinion of many experts, the Isle of Wight was the most likely target for the Armada, it was assumed the Spaniards would seize the island as their base of operations and invade the mainland from there. And although, in fact, King Philip had decreed the Kent side of the Thames estuary as the principal goal, the Isle of Wight had indeed been selected as the secondary objective, should the first plan miscarry.

Thus one might have imagined that its commander, Sir George Carey, would have been accorded some degree of priority in obtaining reinforcements as the Armada crisis mounted, but this hardly seemed to be the case. For the first time in the history of the militia, a degree of mobility had been agreed upon, and so the Isle of Wight was entitled to request extra troops from the Hampshire mainland, where the Earl of Sussex commanded.

Somewhat grudgingly, these were eventually supplied, but the so-called trained bands were hardly to Sir George's liking. They were, he complained, '– a band of men termed trained who I find rather so in name than in deed.' The Isle of Wight, he added, was at least as strategically important as Portsmouth, if not more so, and yet there seemed little appreciation of the fact. 'The Earl of Sussex yet continuing to give out that as a good cook may be his own carver, so he will have all the trained bands to Portsmouth.'

It was a long and hard struggle which the island's commander waged to ensure his territory was adequately supplied with armaments and men. At an earlier stage, after a disappointing response from the authorities in London, he had written testily to Sir Francis Walsingham, 'If this place be of so small importance to be thought worthy of no better provision, having discharged my duty in declaration of my wants, I will perform what I may with my small strength, and wish better success than I have reason to expect.'

Despite local friction of this nature, together with constant haggling over costs and various time-wasting details (in Northamptonshire the colour of the militia's coats had still not been decided, let alone the coats made, only six weeks before the Armada mobilization) the land forces had been slowly licked into shape. The fact that most of them only trained for an hour or two twice a week and rarely had firing practice, or that the cavalry seldom if ever exercised in more than small local groups, must have placed the English at a tremendous disadvantage in the face of Spain's invading army of professionals, but none the less, a Spanish spy, reporting on the preparations for the defence of London, declared that the 6,000 men who drilled there regularly were 'certainly very good troops, considering they are recruits, and they are very well armed.'

Not that the commander of the navy placed much faith in the land forces. It was to be hoped, Lord Howard declared to Lord Burghley, that his men were the first to encounter the Spaniards, 'for I fear me a little sight of the enemy will fear the land men much.'

Had the Spaniards succeeded in getting ashore it would have been the trained bands they first encountered, their high degree of discipline being an essential factor. The authorities were determined to avoid at all costs the sort of gadarene rush to the beaches described thus by an observer of previous alarums. 'Myself, I can remember when upon the firing of the beacons the country people, forthwith, ran down to the seaside, some with clubs, some with picked staves and pitchforks, all unarmed, and they that were best appointed were but with a bill, a bow and a sheaf of arrows, no captain appointed to direct, lead or order them.'

By April of 1588 it had been decided that if the beacons were to blaze again there would be no such disorganization. To guard the entire coastline adequately was clearly an impossibility, although until that time it had been the standard policy. Now the decision was made to concentrate defence at a series of strategic points, notably at ports. So the pick of the militia was detailed to form protective units for all the main ports of the south and south-west, as well as Yarmouth, Harwich and Milford Haven. Other troops were to be assembled inland to form a strategic reserve.

Nearly 400 years later, when the threat of invasion was

almost as acute, from the Germans this time, General Montgomery decided on an identical strategy. When he took command in southern England in 1942, the accepted doctrine was that every foot of coastline should be defended, but as he discovered, the defence had no depth and left far too few troops for counter-attack. Accordingly, like his Tudor predecessors, he pulled many of his men back from the beaches and held them poised in compact bodies, ready to retaliate.

Spanish troops fighting their way inland in 1588 would, in theory, have found themselves advancing through a wasteland of scorched fields and fire-blackened buildings. The order was that if a landing could not be contained, the retreating foot militia were to keep some six or seven miles ahead of the invaders, burning as they retreated. Cavalry were to harass the enemy at every opportunity, the object being to slow them down until a 'grosse' army could be assembled for the counter-attack.

To avoid the confusion of past emergencies, the authorities issued strict instructions that only enrolled men, under the direction of their captains, were to report at the designated assembly sites once the alarm was raised. And when that happened, strategic bridges and fords were to be put under guard, while no man in any coastal town or village was to be allowed to leave, under pain of death.

With barriers of logs and chains to seal off main roads and the approaches to towns and cities, the situation must have been very similar to that in 1940, when the Germans were hourly expected. Then, too, such primitive defences were optimistically devised in many instances, and in a few extreme cases, pikes were even pressed into service for lack of other weapons.

Despite the cries of anguish at increased taxes, the nation as a whole eventually responded moderately well to the threat of the Armada. Voluntary contributions of arms and armour came from many sources, and such, indeed, was the rush to purchase armour (even Sir Francis Walsingham, sick and ageing, ordered a new set) that prices rocketed and manufacturer's could charge almost what they liked.

Horses were also at a premium, and anyone with a few strong animals, fit to carry cavalrymen, could make a small fortune.

But the tax burdens under which the nation groaned were for more than armour and horses. The improvement of defences at such vulnerable locations as the Isle of Wight and key ports had required a huge outlay, and there was, too, the need to fortify potential invasion sites, a large number of which had been identified in the second of the two surveys conducted as the Spanish threat grew.

This report, drawn up in 1585, had suggested that a determined enemy could put troops ashore in just about every maritime county, and although in the ensuing three years a good deal was done to counter this, the lord lieutenant of Hampshire, for one, was still complaining about his inadequately protected coastline shortly before the Armada arrived.

By that time, the newly-agreed mobility of the county militias had enabled the creation of a plan whereby the Spanish ships were shadowed by a growing force of troops as they made their slow way up the Channel. Each inland shire adjacent to a maritime county was ordered to supply men to its sea-bordered neighbour once certain key beacons were fired – Wiltshire troops to Hampshire, for example, those from Somerset to Devon or Dorset, depending on the degree of danger.

The beacon network which spread the Armada alarm the length of the land was of antique vintage but, by 1588, of somewhat limited value. The system had become increasingly susceptible to false alarms, so that an involved method of checking had been devised, so involved that, contrary to long-held belief, the Armada warning seems to have crawled rather than flown across the land. In London, it was over three days after the Spanish fleet had first been sighted before Robert Cary and the Earl of Cumberland got the news and set off to find a ship. In Huntingdonshire it was the day after that when it was first learned by the lord lieutenant there, Oliver Cromwell's grandfather, Sir Henry Cromwell.

If it took that long to travel barely half the length of the land, the Armada would have been almost out of English waters before the far north country even heard of its arrival off Cornwall.

The importance of a secure beacon system had been demonstrated exactly two years earlier when a group of Catholic renegades prepared a plan to fire the Hampshire beacons and in the ensuing tumult, to raid the homes of well-known Protestant landowners and liberate prisoners in Winchester jail. The plot had been foiled and no beacon burned on that occasion, but some time previously a false alarm originating on the Hampshire coast reached Berkshire, 'and stirred all our shire,' in the words of that county's irate lord lieutenant. He was even more incensed when he discovered that the watchers at the Portsdown beacon who gave the alarm had failed to take any action when they realized their mistake, thus causing the militia of two counties to be alerted.

The Portsdown watch must have been particularly 'beacon happy' because some time later they offended again, on this occasion mistaking an attempt to smoke out badgers for a signal from the neighbouring beacon.

Owing to such false alarms, by the date of the Armada, the 'substantial, honest persons' recruited as watchers were not, in theory, permitted to fire a single beacon until a local Justice of the Peace had verified the situation. At coastal locations this could be done visually, but inland the justices were required to send a messenger to the previous beacon to discover why it had been lit.

With such a painstaking system it is easy to understand why more than three days elapsed between the firing of the first beacon in Cornwall and the raising of the alarm among Sir Henry Cromwell's militia in Huntingdonshire.

But no matter how detailed, how well organized the preparations to withstand the Spaniards, the fear of a 'fifth column', composed of English Catholics, was always at the back of the authorities' minds. Events would prove that most Englishmen of that faith rallied to their country's cause just like everyone else when the Armada appeared, but in those long months of waiting, no chances could be taken. Many Catholics had been stripped of their personal weapons and armour as early as 1586, but as the threat from Spain grew more concrete, the most influential among them were detained, the majority going to prison but a fortunate few finding themselves in the Bishop of Ely's palace.

Numerous of their number escaped detention, however, simply by going into hiding, while others benefited from the slackness of local officals. Early in 1588 the commissioners for recusants in Staffordshire found themselves severely reprimanded for failing even to draw up a list of such people in their county.

The Catholic campaign against English Protestantism was orchestrated from his exile in Europe by Cardinal Allen, the

erstwhile head of an Oxford college. He it was who urged the
Vatican and the Spanish king to believe that Catholics in
England, particularly those of ancient and noble family, merely
awaited the signal before leading the nation in revolt against
Queen Elizabeth.

This was strongly stressed to members of the Armada, but, in
fact, it was quite untrue and typified Spain's ill-conceived
propaganda.

So far as the English were concerned, threats against the life of
the queen which emerged from Catholic Europe were completely
counter-productive, as Richard Leigh, a Catholic priest pointed
out to Don Bernardino de Mendoza, the Spanish ambassador in
Paris. Such threats, he told the ambassador, merely angered
Elizabeth's subjects, so that 'some with ire, some with fear, but all
sorts, almost without exception, resolved to venture their lives for
the withstanding of all manner of conquest.'

Spanish attempts to infiltrate Catholic priests into England
were also criticized by Richard Leigh – the men chosen were
frequently quite unsuitable for the task.

'The rashness of divers coming secretly into this realm and
professing themselves to be priests, many of them being both very
young, unlearned and of light behaviour, hath done great harm to
the goodness of our common cause,' Leigh lamented.

The doubt cast on the loyalty of English Catholics was just one
aspect of the complex psychological battle waged between Spain
and England in the run-up to the Armada. For several months the
Spanish propaganda machine had been trumpeting throughout
Europe details of the awesome fleet assembling at Lisbon, but as
England's preparations matured, it was soon possible for Lord
Burghley to counter with a message to Mendoza in Paris.
England, he cautioned, had never been more ready, its militia
never before armed and trained as now, the nation as a whole
never more responsive to danger, never more generous with funds
and armour. Should any invader appear, 20,000 men could be
assembled at any point of attack within forty-eight hours.

If they had not known it before, the Spanish diplomats who
handled Burghley's message must have come to realize that the
Armada enterprise was to be no fiesta.

6 The Waiting Game

Towards the end of June, soon after the bulk of the Armada had been forced into Corunna, the English received reports of Spanish ships in the vicinity of the Scilly Isles, and set forth to investigate. But once more the weather played false, so that within a day or two they were back at Plymouth.

Had they reached their destination they might have found the voyage rewarding, because there were indeed Spanish vessels there, more than a dozen of them. They were victims of the Corunna storm and far from playing some trick on the rest of the Armada, as King Philip had suspiciously suggested, they had, in fact, followed his instructions implicity. Having failed to reach the safety of the harbour they had been driven willy-nilly before the storm as far as the Scillies, where, true to orders, they waited for the rest of the fleet to join them.

They were in the area for about a week, but by the time Captain John Hawkins was eventually able to cast down there with his squadron, they had turned for home.

The reports which filtered in about those Spanish ships had shown them chasing English barques like pike after minnows, but for some time no one could be sure just why they were there, or in what strength. Patrolling towards the mouth of the Channel, however, an English warship ultimately encountered an Irish boat with just three men and a boy aboard. The Irishmen reported that five other crewmen had been taken aboard one of eighteen large Spanish warships which they had met some fifty miles south-west of the Scillies. Their barque itself had been taken in tow, but at night in rough seas the tow-cable parted and they had escaped.

That was the kind of evidence the English had been hoping to discover.

'This did assure us greatly,' Lord Howard informed Sir Francis Walsingham, 'that the Spanish fleet was broken by the storm.'

That news must have brought relief to the Court, not least to Walsingham, since as head of the Secret Service, he would have been concerned by the sudden dearth of information following the Armada's departure from Lisbon. In the preceding fifteen months he had received the largest sum ever granted by Queen Elizabeth for intelligence activities, and had spent some of his own money too. 'Knowledge is never too dear,' he would declare.

Thus his 'intelligencers' had been able to supply reports on Spain's every move – until the Spanish ships put to sea and seemed, after the Biscay storm, to disappear.

To the queen, Lord Howard's information suggested one thing above all others – there was money to be saved. With the Armada scattered, she argued, the project must at least have been postponed, if not entirely abandoned. Let three first-class ships of war be laid up, therefore, and their crews paid off.

To the Lord Admiral that was a most alarming suggestion, and he reacted accordingly. Already, he protested, he had been forced to lay up several ships owing to the great amount of sickness in the fleet, he could not dispense with three more, three first-class ships at that.

Reluctantly, Queen Elizabeth was forced to accept the logic of his case.

Although parsimonious by nature, the queen could hardly be blamed for seeking economies at every opportunity, because the nation's financial situation had seldom been more serious. Foreign loans were almost impossible to come by, with the great capital market of Antwerp under Spanish control, the bankers of Lyons not prepared to lend any more, and Italian bankers supporting Catholic Spain.

Furthermore, customs revenues, a major source of government income, had plummeted as the result of the disastrous collapse of trade. England's credit-worthiness was practically nil.

None the less, the queen's tight fist was a major concern to the navy, and with victuals in permanent short supply, and men unpaid for weeks on end, it was no wonder that Lord Howard should appeal to Lord Burghley, with a note of desperation in his plea, 'For the love of God, let her Majesty not now care for charges.'

The navy's victualling problems were a constant worry to the

Lord Admiral, and had been since crews were remustered in early spring, leading him to observe tartly in one despatch that the queen's father, King Henry VIII, would never have allowed ships to sail with such limited supplies.

Indeed, the suspicion began to grow in Howard's mind that the Spaniards planned to turn the problem to their own advantage. 'I am verily persuaded,' he told Walsingham, 'they mean nothing else but to linger it out upon their own coast, until they understand that we have spent our victuals here.'

It was no comfort to him that part of the problem resulted from the sheer size to which the fleet had expanded. By the early summer of 1588, the navy had been reinforced by armed merchantmen and other auxiliaries, so that something approaching 100 ships were involved.

All through June, and virtually up to the time the Armada arrived in the Channel at the end of July, Lord Howard was having to nag about the shortage of supplies.

'We have now but 18 days victual, and there is none to be gotten in all this country,' he reported to Lord Burghley from Plymouth in early June. He had been forced, he announced, to commandeer rice from a Hamburg ship because of short rations; '– there is here the gallantest company of captains, soldiers and mariners that I think ever was seen in England. It were a pity they should lack meat when they are so desirous to spend their lives in her Majesty's service.'

Two weeks later, the attack was switched to Walsingham, 'Sir,' Howard expostulated, 'I will never go again to such a place of service but I will carry my victuals with me, and not trust to careless men behind me.' Thankfully, he added, there was no sign of mutiny yet, '– for I see men kindly handled will bear want and run through fire and water.' Supply one month's rations, he pleaded, and the fleet would make them last 'very near three months'.

When July arrived, with still no sign of victualling ships from London, there grew among the senior commanders at Plymouth a real fear that some disaster might have overtaken those ships. 'I hope shortly we shall hear of our victuals for the wind doth now serve them,' the Lord Admiral declared. 'I pray God all be well with them, for if any chance should come to them we should be in a most miserable case.'

Finally, two days after the abortive attempt to reach the

Scillies, fifteen victualling ships arrived and the navy could contemplate a prolonged spell at sea in their search for the Armada. So anxious was Lord Howard to seek out those storm-driven Spaniards off the Scillies, in fact, that many of his ships had to leave without their full rations.

Although Lord Howard's expanded fleet included a number of volunteers, other vessels had been supplied as the result of levies upon coastal towns, levies seldom met in full and usually executed amid cries of anguished protest.

Southampton, for example, called upon to provide two ships and a pinnace, declared plaintively, '– finding the charge to amount to five hundred pounds or thereabouts, we see it not possible how the same (no, not the fourth part thereof) can be levied among us, in respect of the disability and poverty of the town.'

The collapse of trade was pleaded by town after town, Ipswich, East Bergholt, Kingston-upon-Hull, Poole (which added to its list of troubles the activities of pirates at Studland Bay), Lyme Regis and numerous others.

King's Lynn had a different complaint, it had discovered that none of the neighbouring towns such as Blakeney, Cley and Wiveton were prepared to pay a portion of the levy. 'We also sent to the town of Wells,' the mayor reported, 'a town very well furnished with shipping, within which there be many rich men inhabiting, but they have denied altogether to contribute to our charge.'

These levies did, indeed, appear to be imposed in a highly arbitrary manner, because Exeter also complained that although it and Topsham had been picked on, about a dozen neighbouring places, including Exmouth, Sidmouth, Teignmouth and Tiverton had escaped.

Weymouth was another town which appealed to have the burden of its levy shared 'with some township adjoining', and the Suffolk boroughs of Orford, Dunwich and Aldeburgh demanded that Woodbridge and owners of country estates in the vicinity should also pay a share.

Despite the cataract of complaints and objections, the number of ships ultimately forthcoming seemed to amount to perhaps two-thirds of what was demanded, probably about as much as the authorities would have hoped for, even though, to the indignation of Lord Howard, some vessels were sent to the fleet with neither victuals or even water.

In any event, as various of the queen's ships were quick to claim, it was they and not the auxiliaries who bore the brunt of the Armada battles and who inflicted the greatest damage on the enemy.

Those redesigned and rebuilt royal ships were the result of a stewardship by John Hawkins which also produced in the naval dockyards a dramatic decrease in corruption and far greater efficiency. A year or two before the Armada, Hawkins claimed to be saving the queen £1,000 a year, the equivalent of four new ships.

But, inevitably, he made enemies, both among the shipwrights in the yards, and those managers whom he had superseded, so that there were rumours at Court of sharp practice, corruption, even. Worse still, there were whispers of poorly executed work.

Fortunately for John Hawkins, his principal champion was the Lord Admiral himself, who dismissed the critics with the scornful assertion that they would be proved 'notable liars' when the fleet was put to the test of battle.

And when sniping began after the *Hope* put in to port with a leak, Howard declared roundly to Walsingham, 'I think there never was so many of the prince's ships so long abroad and in such seas – with so few leaks.' The royal vessels were in far better condition than the rest, 'for when the weather hath been bad and rough, the most part of all the navy have besought that I and the rest of her Majesty's ships would bear less sail, for they could not endure it, when we made no reckoning of it.'

It was as well those royal ships had been rendered so sturdy because, as the Lord Admiral had indicated in his despatch, July storms were battering the fleet day after day as it patrolled in the Sleeve, the western end of the Channel, following its departure from Plymouth.

His crews, he reported, 'have danced as lustily as the gallantest dancers in the Court' aboard their pitching, rolling vessels.

'I know not what weather you have had there,' he declared in another message to Walsingham, 'but there never was any such summer seen here on the sea.'

But it was not the weather which was the navy's main problem at that stage, illness among the crews was a far greater worry.

'God of his mercy keep us from sickness, for we fear that more than any hurt the Spaniards will do. We must now man ourselves again, for we have cast many overboard,' he was soon forced to report.

Sickness was a permanent hazard in the cramped, foetid conditions of those Elizabethan warships. Healthy recruits would go aboard and be dead within twenty-four hours, so virulent were the fevers there.

Aboard Lord Howard's flagship, the *Ark*, was his personal surgeon, William Clowes, author of the first book in English on military surgery, but medical care in the fleet as a whole was hard to find. Doctors and surgeons could not be recruited by means of the press-gang, and although their charters required them to provide service on request, all too often those selected sought to evade duty by paying less-skilled men to take their places. Medicine seems, in any event, to have been a poorly regarded trade since, in the militia, the pay of a surgeon was no more than that of a trumpeter, and the navy was probably similar.

For two weeks and more the fleet patrolled in the Sleeve, speaking every vessel sighted in the attempt to glean information about the Armada, but they were tactically ill-sited there, as Sir Francis Drake had warned the Lord Admiral at more than one meeting. There was too little sea-room so that if the Spaniards suddenly emerged from the Bay of Biscay, they would have the weather gauge and the English would be too cramped to outsail them and gain the wind.

Eventually, the vice-admiral put his views in writing and that seemed to produce the desired result because shortly afterwards the fleet moved further west, with John Hawkins and his squadron of twenty or so vessels patrolling on the starboard flank, out towards the Isles of Scilly, Drake and his similarly-sized force on the port station off Ushant, and Howard, with the main part of the navy, guarding the centre.

Just before leaving Plymouth, the Lord Admiral had received further instructions from the Privy Council, his bitter protest over their change of mind on the original plan to attack the Armada on its own coast had had its effect, now he was informed he was free to decide strategy himself, subject only to the approval of his council-of-war.

After day upon day of fruitless patrolling, and with disease rife in his squadron, Francis Drake was once more for taking the initiative and making for Spain at the first opportunity, but there were reservations among some of the captains because victuals were short again, barely sufficient, it was calculated, to reach the coast of Spain, let alone return.

The debate was academic, however, since the unceasing southerly gales made it quite impossible to set a course for Spain – there was nothing to do but watch and wait.

It was a period of considerable strain, particularly for Lord Howard. His ships could not locate the Spanish in such continuously foul weather, and just as Nelson was to be carped at, 200 years later, for his failure to find the French fleet before the battle of the Nile, so Howard's critics were at work, joined, it would seem, by Queen Elizabeth herself. Her secretary, Walsingham, hinted that her Majesty thought more might be done in the way of 'espials', the use of reconnaissance vessels to sniff out the enemy.

It was a further irritant to the Lord Admiral, and he responded accordingly. 'We are here to small purpose for this great service if that hath not been thought of,' he declared sharply. 'There hath been no day but that there hath been pinnaces, Spanish carvels, flyboats and of all sort sent out to discover them.'

In those fierce southerlies, he pointed out, his warships could not get near enough to the Spanish coast to capture local fishermen and find out from them what had happened to the Armada (the usual tactic) – 'and to send some of our fisherboats to discover there, they would do as much good as to send an oyster boat of Billingsgate, for neither can they sail anything or (be) able to bear the seas.'

On 17 July, however, came the weather change that Drake and the more aggressive members of the fleet had long looked for, the wind went round to the north – a fair wind for Spain.

After a lengthy council-of-war it was agreed, the fleet would set course for Corunna.

For thirty-six hours the English ships ran under full sail across the Bay of Biscay, but then, when they were little more than a hundred miles from their destination, the north wind faltered and died, to be succeeded by a hard-blowing southwester. In the teeth of such weather there was nothing for it but to reduce sail, turn and run, all the way back to the shelter of Plymouth harbour.

A foul wind for Spain, but to the Armada, now reunited and
refreshed at Corunna, a fair wind for England.

7   *End of an Interlude*

Three days after the English turned back, the Armada began to
work out of port once more. For nearly a week beforehand,
tents had been set up on an island in Corunna harbour and,
again emphasizing the sacred nature of the mission, by the day
of departure every man in the fleet, Spaniards, Portuguese,
Italians, Flemings and a motley assembly of other races, had
received absolution, the ceremonies conducted by priests from
among the 180 men of religion who sailed with the Armada.

As she had done on leaving the Tagus, once again Medina
Sidonia's flagship, the *San Martin*, carried at her foremast the
royal ensign, together with the red and white flag of the Spanish
empire. At her mainmast hung the Armada's own standard,
which had been consecrated with antique pageantry in Lisbon
cathedral and presented to the duke one month before the fleet
left port there. The great standard bore upon it the portrayal of
a crucifix between the figures of Our Lady and St Mary
Magdalene, together with an exhortation, *Exsurge domine et
vindica causa tuam* – 'Arise, oh Lord, and avenge thy cause'.

A colourful spectacle those departing ships must have
presented because in addition to the red and white empire flag
which every vessel flew, and the crimson cross adorning many a
sail, each ship also bore the emblem of its native province,
together with the flags of whatever men of noble blood it
carried. And since this group included nearly 150 gentlemen
adventurers (attended by more than 400 servants) a veritable
forest of flags must have flowered as the Armada worked its way
out of harbour.

Equally exotic would have been the peacock garb of many

who sailed that day. In the atmosphere of optimism which had prevailed in Lisbon as the fleet prepared itself, credit had been easy to come by since all were expected to return from England loaded with booty. Thus, 'the soldiers and gentlemen that come on this voyage are very richly appointed,' reported Gilbert Lee, who arrived home from Spain just two weeks before the Armada reached English waters.

How richly appointed may be gauged from the following list of items subsequently taken from Spanish prisoners – a pair of breeches of yellow satin, drawn out with silver cloth; a leather jerkin, perfumed with amber and laid over with gold and silver lace; a coloured cloak trimmed with gold lace; a pair of breeches of cloth of gold; black velvet breeches; blue satin breeches; silk breeches with gold lace; blue velvet hose with gold and silver lace; a jerkin of wrought velvet lined with taffeta.

But if fine clothes were easily obtained on credit by individual members of the Armada, the Spanish government itself had been extremely hard-pressed to finance the enterprise, funds, in fact, were just about as difficult for the Spaniards to raise as for the impecunious English.

The Duke of Medina Sidonia had been made fully aware of this by King Philip in one of the numerous warnings on different aspects of the project issued to him by the monarch. He was to take the greatest care of the money carried by the fleet, the duke was told, 'You know how much trouble it has cost to collect it, and the necessity from which we are suffering.'

Small wonder that Philip should be looking with anxious envy towards the Vatican and the one million gold ducats to be had from there if, but only if, the Armada venture succeeded.

In fact, of course, not only was the Vatican largesse never received, but much of the money carried by the Spanish fleet either went to the bottom in sunken ships, or was captured by the English.

As the enterprise was slowly shaped, the Spanish king, who was sixty-one, had given it daily attention at the remote, granite Escurial palace, which he himself had created a wearying thirty miles south of Madrid. To the Spanish people he was Philip the Prudent, but his prudence seems to have been less a cautious trait than a chronic inability to make decisions. 'Time and I are one,' he would declare as his ministers earnestly sought his final word on vexatious problems, but, in fact, it was procrastination he was more akin to, that thief of time.

On the matter of the Armada, however, he had displayed uncharacteristic urgency, probably because the mission itself seemed so obviously necessary and so obviously in God's interest. Throughout the previous year he had nagged and bullied the Marquis of Santa Cruz to hasten preparations along, his frustration mounting with each new excuse from the old admiral, genuine as it might be.

Now, with the Duke of Medina Sidonia replacing Santa Cruz, Philip had drawn the strands of the operation even more firmly into his own hands, often working till dawn in his determination to ensure its success. Only once in his life had he himself experienced a battle, and this so distressed him that he appears to have decided in future to command by the remotest of remote control – by letter – even though he informed Medina Sidonia, by letter, that it was only the constant pressure of State business which kept him from leading the Armada personally.

Had he indeed filled that role, the Duke of Parma might have found it expedient to be more communicative than he was with Medina Sidonia, in which case the prospects for success would have been considerably greater, but it was not to be.

Instead, Philip brooded constantly on the impending operation, with little, it seemed, escaping his attention. The duke had been warned what tactics the English were likely to adopt in view of their superior fire-power – they would aim at the water-line. The Armada, on the other hand, was to seek to grapple as always, and greedy commanders were not to jeopardize the venture by breaking formation in search of booty.

The fleet was also to proceed up the Channel by way of the English rather than the French coast because of the danger of shoals along the latter – a strange decision since, in fact, the French side of the Channel was no more hazardous than the English and would have offered a better chance of avoiding detection.

Medina Sidonia had also been advised on the plan to pursue if problems arose over the rendezvous with the Duke of Parma – the Isle of Wight was to be seized in that event, with the Spanish ships entering by the east channel, which was wider than the west.

In mustering his troops, the Armada's commander was to ensure no tricks were played, otherwise he would be paying for non-existent men; and when the juncture with Parma was achieved, 6,000 of those troops were to be assigned to his command, or as many as could be spared should numbers have been depleted by combat.

Thus King Philip's instructions flowed on: rationing, health at sea, piety of the men, condition of the ships, nothing, large or small, appeared to go unconsidered.

In addition to the stream of harassing orders received from the king, and the chaos he discovered in Lisbon, Medina Sidonia had found himself confronting one other vexing problem before the Armada's original sailing, the poor state of relations between the Portuguese and Spanish.

It was only eight years earlier that Spain had annexed Portugal, causing the Portuguese monarch, Antonio, to flee to England. Since then there had been nothing but trouble for his people, their ships had become as fair game for attacks by English privateers as were Spanish vessels, and with the lucrative trade with Spain's colonies all but halted by preparations for the Armada, Portugal's commerce was quite as badly affected as that of Spain. And, as a final provocation to the increasingly sullen populace, the bulk of the Portuguese grain harvest had been diverted to the Spanish fleet at artificially low prices.

But, in spite of this bad blood between Spanish and Portuguese elements of the Armada, in spite of concern about victuals and water supplies, and in spite, above all, of Medina Sidonia's grave reservations about the entire venture, by the afternoon of 22 July the fleet was at sea once more, and although it then had to endure several frustrating hours of dead calm, eventually the wind picked up from the south-east and it was on its way.

For the first three days of the resumed voyage the weather was good, but with the cargo boats as cumbersome as ever, a lengthy journey was clearly in prospect.

Across the Bay of Biscay the *San Martin* led the Armada, the rest of the fleet carefully observing the order not to precede the flagship. (Later, after the stress of combat, a captain would ignore this command, and be hanged for his disobedience.)

Each evening, after shipboys had congregated on deck to sing *Ave Maria* – as they chanted *Buenos Dias* at dawn – every vessel in the fleet would report to the *San Martin* to learn the password for the night, part of the elaborate procedure carried out at the king's behest.

The duke's instructions to the Armada, founded on those of King Philip, including the positioning of each ship in the fleet, where to make for in emergency, and the procedure to ensure enemy vessels did not insinuate themselves. There were also orders concerning the behaviour of crews – no blaspheming on such a holy mission, no gambling, the suspension of all feuds until one month beyond the completion of the Armada's task, no friction between soldiers and seamen, no truckle beds aboard (that was ignored) and no women.

This last command, if not ignored, seems to have been complied with only tardily because a few days before the fleet left Lisbon, some 600 women were reported to have been flushed out and deported from the city. Even then, at least one woman, a German, sailed with the Armada, she being taken prisoner by the English.

And if contemporary accounts are to be believed, some of the most resourceful among that tribe of banished females actually hired ships and followed, only giving up when Biscay storms drove them ashore in France.

In those early days out in the Bay of Biscay, the weather was as good as anything the Armada could have desired, but the snail-like progress of the fleet was a great irritation to its commander. 'If three or four of our ships had cared to clap on sail, even though they were not very swift,' he reported to King Philip, 'they might have arrived at the mouth of the Channel by Monday, the 25th.

'But I in this galleon could only sail as fast as the scurviest ship in the fleet – verily some of them are dreadfully slow – so I was obliged, anxious as I was to get forward, to tarry on the way.'

That tardiness was unfortunate because by the fourth day, 26 July, the weather was beginning to change, with the sea rising and the wind going around to west-north-west. That was too much for one of the galleys, and, leaking badly, she limped away towards the French coast as a sudden heavy rainstorm struck.

The next day the wind grew stronger and the seas steeper, so that by midnight the stern gallery of the *San Christobal*, flagship of the Castile squadron, had been carried clean away and the Armada's formation began to break up.

'It was the most cruel night ever seen,' Medina Sidonia later reported to King Philip, although, in fact, it seems to have been a typical Biscay storm, briefly violent but doubtless extremely alarming – and uncomfortable – for a novice mariner highly prone to seasickness.

By dawn, forty vessels were missing, including the Armada's three remaining galleys, each of which had also run for the French coast, where one was wrecked. Among the other absentees was the *Santa Anna*, flagship of the Biscay squadron, which for some inexplicable reason ran under storm canvas about 90° off-course, eventually reaching Le Havre and taking no further part in operations.

As soon as the situation was verified and the Armada's position seventy-five leagues south-west of the Scillies had been checked, search pinnaces were despatched to seek out the missing vessels, and after an anxious twenty-four hours, one of them returned with the news that most of the lost ships had been rounded up in the vicinity of the Lizard by the commander of the Andalusian squadron, Don Pedro de Valdes.

Unfortunately for Medina Sidonia, that group of vessels was sighted by Captain Thomas Fleming, master of the *Golden Hind*, as they waited for the rest of the Armada. Fleming mistook them for the entire fleet and sped back to Plymouth to raise the alarm, arriving on the afternoon of Friday, 29 July, to find Sir Francis Drake engaged in that legendary game of bowls on the Hoe. Whether Drake did indeed declare there was time to finish the game and beat the Spaniards too is uncertain, although such a remark would certainly accord with his character. What is beyond debate is the invaluable amount of time Captain Fleming's sighting gained for the English.

Conversely, it was a stroke of cruel luck for the Spaniards that their approach should be detected so early, but it was just one of the many blows of misfortune which were to assail the Duke of Medina Sidonia – decidedly he was not the sort of lucky commander which, a couple of centuries later, Napoleon was to value above all the rest.

Captain Fleming's news had come as a surprise, and about the time the English commanders were digesting it, the coast of Cornwall presented itself to the Armada, a dark outline on the northern horizon. At that moment, the sacred banner was run up the mainmast of the *San Martin*, a salvo of gunfire echoed across the grey sea, and the entire ship's crew knelt to give thanks and to beseech victory.

By the following wet and murky morning, the fleet was near

enough to the coast to see the Lizard beacon start to send its
smoky warning billowing along the clifftops, and it was around
this time that a pinnace reached the flagship with a valuable
cargo, the crew of an English fishing boat. According to the later
evidence of Pedro de Valdes, the Andalucian commander, the
fishermen reported that the English fleet was still at Plymouth,
which raised in the minds of the Spaniards the exciting
possibility of attacking the English at anchor. Thus a
council-of-war was hastily assembled.

The most experienced seaman among the assembly, the
elderly Juan de Recalde, vice-admiral of the Biscay squadron,
had long favoured the seizure of such a port as Plymouth and
had written to King Philip to stress the need to do so —
complaining in the same letter about the way in which sons of
gentlemen were being given command of troops over the heads
of experienced professional officers.

Also in favour of an attack on Plymouth was said to be Don
Alonzo de Leyva, the most illustrious figure in that entire
glittering galaxy which sailed with the Armada. He had been
Captain General of the Milanese Cavalry, a post of great
seniority, until resigning that command to participate in King
Philip's enterprise, and his charisma had drawn as volunteers to
his ship the flower of Spain's noble youth. But like a number of
other commanders around the council table that morning, de
Leyva was a soldier, not a seaman, and thus the complexities of
a sea-borne assault must have been less obvious to him.

In any event, although the idea of such an attack appears at
some point in the discussion to have found a good deal of
favour, it was eventually rejected, partly, at least, because of the
confined approaches to Plymouth harbour, where no more than
three ships could enter at a time.

Although the Spaniards were not to know it, the debate was,
of course, entirely academic since Captain Fleming's warning of
the previous afternoon had given the English time enough to get
out of port.

What was eventually decided was that a course should be set
for the Isle of Wight, off which the Armada would wait until
news of Parma's readiness was received. The problem facing
Medina Sidonia was that for weeks he had heard nothing from
the general, despite sending off pinnaces to France to seek
information. Another pinnace would have to be despatched

once they got further into the Channel, because, as the duke declared in a letter to King Philip, the entire success of the project depended upon Parma's absolute preparedness, so that 'at the moment of my arrival he should sally with his fleet without causing me to wait a minute.'

The Armada's commander was to be grievously disillusioned on that matter.

After the council had ended and its participants returned to their various ships, the fleet edged slowly along the Cornish coast, past Falmouth and on towards Fowey, limited by the *urcas* to a speed barely above a man's walking pace. While ashore, at perhaps the same pace, the beacons began to thread the alarm across England.

When that southwesterly wind which brought the Armada out of Corunna had driven Lord Howard's ships back to Plymouth, all the English admiral's problems bore in upon him once more. Those long, fruitless days of patrolling empty seas had taken a grim toll among his men, crews were remustered yet again, more pressed men found, various futile attempts made to rid the ships themselves of the diseases which were claiming so many lives.

Shortage of victuals provided the usual worry, particularly since, to the Lord Admiral's anger, auxiliaries were still arriving with neither food nor water. There was, in fact, barely a penny to be found for anything.

'I cannot stir out but I have an infinite number hanging on my shoulders for money,' Howard complained to Walsingham. While at the same time, Lord Henry Seymour, commander of the squadron assigned to guard the approaches to the Thames estuary, was protesting that his men had received no pay for sixteen weeks and that 'what with fair means and foul, I have enough to do to keep them from mutiny.'

Of all the problems confronting the English, however, none was more acute when the Armada's proximity was first reported than the state of wind and tide at Plymouth. As the *Golden Hind* carried Captain Fleming into harbour to raise the alarm, a brisk breeze was blowing directly onshore and a strong tide soon began to flow, so that Lord Howard's ships were quite powerless to move, and remained so for several hours.

That the Spanish were so close was a surprise to the Lord Admiral and his colleagues, they believed their opponents still to be at Corunna, and were planning to blockade the port there, while at the same time sending a detachment of thirty sail to intercept the treasure fleet on its annual return to Spain.

Their surprise would have turned to consternation had the Armada succeeded in bottling them up at Plymouth at that moment. How altered, therefore, might the Spanish case have been had those scurvy slow sailers clapped on extra sail during those first days out of Corunna. And, indeed, how might the history of England, Spain, and perhaps the entire Western world have been influenced had that Biscay storm not broken up the Armada and caused its waiting vanguard to be discovered off the Lizard.

That discovery, though, set the trapped English ships warping out of harbour as fast as could be once the tide began to ebb, so that by dawn of 30 July, despite the onshore wind which had blown all night, perhaps half the fleet was anchored to the west of Plymouth in the lee of Rame Head. This was a notable feat of seamanship and it was repeated on the next ebb, when another group of ships worked clear, so that by noon or thereabouts, Lord Howard was able to survey from the deck of the *Ark* a force of more than fifty vessels.

As they beat out to sea against the wind, bearing south towards Eddystone, the damp, misty morning began to give way to an afternoon of thinning rain and broken cloud. And as visibility slowly improved, so the topmen aboard the English ships came gradually to discern the Armada, a dark and sinister mass of shapes fronting the distant coastline, mile after mile of ships there seemed to be, stretching all the way back as far as Fowey.

Then, with increasing numbers of men climbing aloft to view that unique, awesome spectacle, the English fleet itself was briefly visible to the Spaniards as a shaft of watery sun glinted on its sails.

But lowering clouds blanked out the sun once more, making it impossible for either side to gain an accurate impression of the other, and a sudden squall threw a curtain across the water. When it had cleared, the two navies were no longer visible to one another.

8   *The Beacons Burn*

Around nine o'clock the following morning, as the Armada proceeded cautiously up the Channel in battle formation, an English pinnace, the aptly-named *Disdain*, made swiftly towards the towering mass of Spanish ships and fired a single shot. In that fashion, the challenge of Lord Admiral Howard was carried to the Duke of Medina Sidonia – the naval version of throwing down the gauntlet. This gesture, with all its connotations of medieval chivalry, was but one among numerous indications that war at sea was still regarded as an extension of war on land. Even England's Lord Admiral would often refer to his fleet as an army, and certainly the whole Spanish approach to sea combat remained firmly based on the tactics and experience of land fighting.

The dawn of that Sunday, another day of indifferent weather, had found the Armada drawing itself together in a formation reminiscent of a force of troops, with the main weight in the van and strong units of galleons on either flank, the entire deployment generally reported to have formed the shape of a crescent, or perhaps an inverted V.

Intelligence reports available to the Spaniards had suggested that Lord Howard and a strong force of the queen's ships would sail to meet them head-on from the east, while Sir Francis Drake and his squadron of armed merchantmen would attack from the west. The Armada was thus deployed to meet attacks from both directions, its ultimate aim being, as always, to involve the enemy in close-range combat so that troops could storm aboard.

Although in the run-up to this campaign, the Spanish had made strenuous attempts to increase their supply of long-range guns, their efforts were thoroughly belated. The development of naval warfare had received scant attention from Spain's professional militarists, many of whom continued to regard the ship as little more than a floating battlefield where soldiers stood

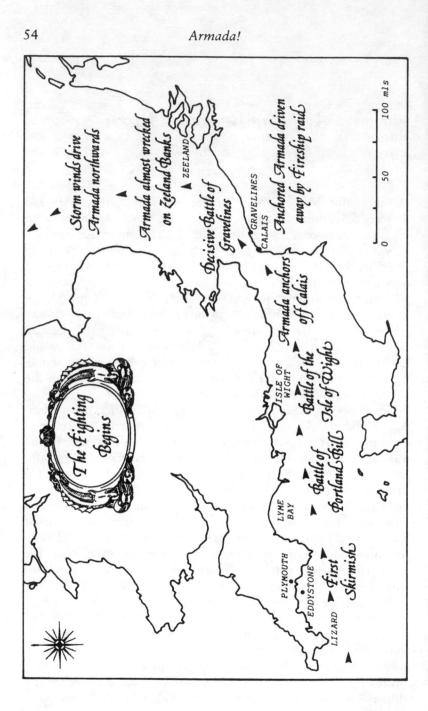

and fought, and the use of heavy guns as a distinctly unchivalrous form of combat.

And while a number of the Armada's senior commanders had valuable sea experience, the army was the predominant element, with soldiers outnumbering sailors by more than two to one throughout the fleet (the reverse of the English navy) and mariners regarded as very much the junior partners in the project.

Ships' captains too were accorded relatively low status, the overall commander of almost every major ship in the Armada being a military man.

With that kind of emphasis it was hardly surprising that in the nine days of sea warfare upon which the curtain was about to rise, the Spaniards should be consistently outsailed.

During the night preceding this opening phase, as the Spanish fleet continued its slow easterly progress, with Polperro and Looe away to port and the dark outline of Rame Head before them, the senior officers aboard the *San Martin* had become uncomfortably aware of enemy vessels towards the Cornish shore, the flickering of lights which suggested warships out of Plymouth and working to gain the wind.

What part of the English fleet was this, they anxiously asked themselves, was it, as some believed, the main body of Sir Francis Drake's force, or merely a handful of decoys?

Daybreak brought the answer, there were just eleven ships in that group, according to Medina Sidonia's later report, including three great galleons which briefly engaged the port flank of the Armada before skilfully tacking to windward and moving out to sea where, through the murk, a much larger English force was descried.

The duke himself reported as many as eighty ships in that force, although that was probably an exaggeration, but when the first attack came, soon after the *Disdain* had issued Lord Howard's challenge, the Spaniards could count at least sixty vessels bearing towards them.

To their surprise, however, the English were approaching in a formation never before experienced in battle, sailing line ahead – in single file, in other words. And the fact that they had somehow got to windward of the Armada led some in that fleet to conjecture that they must be some previously unknown squadron, possibly out of Dartmouth.

The new tactics which Lord Howard's fleet was to employ throughout the campaign were now revealed, because as the long file of vessels approached, each in turn fired a broadside before heeling away beyond range of the Spanish guns, to circle and repeat the process. There was to be no mass attack, the Spaniards could see, with force meeting force, head to head. These gadfly English ships would sting and run. Something entirely original was occurring.

At the tip of one of the two horns of the Armada's formation, at one of the most strategically vital points, therefore, was the *Rata Coronada*, the galleon both commanded and supplied by the illustrious Don Alonzo de Leyva. In the same position on the other flank was the *San Juan*, flagship of the Portuguese squadron, whose commander was the redoubtable Juan de Recalde, veteran of Lepanto and numerous skirmishes with English privateers.

It was as well for the Spanish that such resolute men as de Leyva and Recalde were positioned to receive the first charge of Lord Howard's fleet, because when English guns began to spew their great shot – up to 50 lb in weight – towards the Armada, there was a flinching among some of the captains as they crowded their ships in towards the sheltered centre of the formation in an attempt to get out of range. It was a distinct hint of cowardice in the opinion of some Spanish observers.

But for all that, this great mass of towering ships must have presented a spectacle of awesome intimidation from the decks of the lower-built English vessels, and it almost certainly accounts for the fact that, roar as the cannons might, much of their shot fell short, and precious powder was thus wasted, because many of Lord Howard's ships stood too far off in that first encounter.

Just how much bigger those Armada ships actually were is difficult to establish since Spanish tonnage was measured differently from English. Among the queen's ships were three giants, the *Triumph*, *White Bear* and *Elizabeth Jonas*, all around 1,000 tons, but the average size of the remainder was little more than half that. Certainly the Spanish vessels *looked* bigger, tall ships made taller by their castles fore and aft, so that they gained a significant psychological advantage at first sighting, as was doubtless intended.

As he led his fleet into the attack, Lord Howard had singled out de Leyva's *Rata Coronada* as his target, assuming that by its size and position it must be Medina Sidonia's flagship, and the two engaged in a spirited but seemingly harmless action which terminated when, in Howard's own words, the *Rata* 'was rescued by divers ships of the Spanish army'.

Meantime, Recalde's vessel was in much more serious trouble on the other wing as Drake, in the *Revenge*, led a formidable group of ships against her, a group which included the redoubtable John Hawkins, in the *Victory*, and Martin Frobisher, aboard the *Triumph*.

For some uncertain reason, Recalde's ship had gone about to face Drake's challenge when attacked, whereas the rest of the Spaniards, with the exception of the huge *El Gran Grin*, now leading the Biscay squadron, had done their best to get away. Thus these two were dangerously isolated, so that for an hour or more they were little more than target practice for the English gunners, Recalde's *San Juan* in particular.

If Recalde had hoped by his manoeuvre to tempt Drake into trying to board him, thereby drawing the English into a mêlée in which they might themselves be boarded, he was to be disappointed. The English were showing no inclination at all to fight in the conventional method.

As a number of other Armada ships began to work back against the wind to assist Recalde there was for a while a confused pattern of skirmishing, but then, with the action threatening to carry the English ships leeward of the main body of the Armada, which waited with slackened sails for Recalde to rejoin, Lord Howard broke off the fight. Some forty ships from Plymouth had still to join his fleet, so there was no point in taking risks.

And so the mauled *San Juan* was able to make her way back to the protective centre of the Spanish fleet, her rigging in ribbons, her forestay cut through, and with a couple of cannon shot embedded in her foremast.

On balance, though, the Duke of Medina Sidonia could review this first encounter with reasonable satisfaction; although discipline had faltered when the first shot began to fly, no serious damage had been sustained, and the fleet was intact.

By the end of that day, however, with no intervention whatsoever on the part of the English, two capital ships would be lost to the Armada – the duke was not a lucky commander.

After Lord Howard broke off the action, the commander of the

Andalusian squadron, that same Pedro de Valdes who had
rounded up the scattered Armada ships off the Lizard two days
previously, sent his pinnace to discover the condition of
Recalde's ship. The Biscayan admiral reported himself 'sore
beaten', and requested assistance, but on the way to help, de
Valdes' ship, *Nuestra Senora del Rosario*, collided with another
Andalusian. The harm was not too serious, a damaged spritsail
and crossyard, but it meant that without her full complement of
sail the *Rosario* became difficult to steer, so that within a short
while she had hit another ship, this time shattering her bowsprit
and damaging some of her halyards, the tackle for raising and
lowering sails.

With the rest of the Armada trying, unsuccessfully, to get to
windward of the English, de Valdes got his ship to the lee-side of
his colleagues, lowered sail, and prepared to make repairs.
Earlier he had sent word of his plight to Medina Sidonia and
requested him to wait.

Before the duke could turn his attention to the *Rosario*,
however, an explosion reverberated through the Armada, and
when the smoke had cleared it could be seen that the *San
Salvador*, one of the biggest galleons in the Guipuzcoan
squadron, was ablaze, with her great sterncastle blown clean
away and two of her decks shattered.

The *San Salvador*'s powder magazine had gone up, probably
owing to some wayward spark, although the incident gave birth
to a tribe of fanciful rumours concerning sabotage, treason and
the like. Whatever the cause, it was of special concern to Medina
Sidonia since the Paymaster General was aboard, and with him,
a good deal of the money which the Armada carried. Thus,
while the *San Salvador* drifted helplessly astern and the English
began to stand towards her, the duke turned the *San Martin* in
her direction and fired a signal for the rest of the fleet to follow
suit.

Seeing the Spaniards bearing back towards them, the English
prudently stood off, so that Medina Sidonia's men were able to
get aboard and extinguish the flames, after which, some of the
injured were removed, and the shattered vessel nursed back into
the fleet.

Meanwhile, with the sea beginning to rise and the weather
thickening, repairs were going on aboard the *Rosario*, but she
was a ship as ill-built as she was ill-fated, because as she pitched

and rolled in the steepening seas her foremast, lacking its supporting stays, suddenly broke at deck level and fell on to the mainmast.

Now de Valdes' situation was serious, and an urgent message was despatched to the flagship requesting either a tow or some instructions on how to proceed. At the same time, cannon bellowed from the ship to emphasize her plight.

There are two versions of what happened next, both supplied to the King of Spain, one by de Valdes, the other by the Duke of Medina Sidonia. They differ considerably and one is left to assume that only King Philip's personal knowledge of the two men permitted him to separate fact from fancy.

The version which de Valdes supplied put the duke in a highly unfavourable light. 'Although he was near enough to me and saw in what case I was, and might easily have relieved me, yet he would not do it,' the Andalusian commander roundly declared, 'but even as if we had not been your Majesty's subjects nor employed in your service, discharged a piece to call the fleet together, and followed his course, leaving me comfortless in the sight of the whole fleet, the enemy being but a quarter of a league from me.'

Medina Sidonia's account, almost certainly the more accurate, indicated that far from refusing aid, the crew of the *San Martin* itself had actually got a hawser aboard the *Rosario*, but in the ever-rising sea it had parted.

With shattered masts and no sails, de Valdes' ship had become a useless hulk which no amount of temporary repairs would retrieve, particularly in view of the weather and the approaching night. Thus the difficult but logical decision had been taken to abandon her and sail on.

Medina Sidonia had given this order after his chief tactical adviser had urgently pointed out the danger to the entire Armada which could be caused by lingering with the *Rosario*. This officer was the commander of the galleons of Castile, Don Diego Flores de Valdes, a highly experienced seaman and a cousin of Pedro de Valdes – for whom, it was rumoured, he bore little love.

But despite any personal animosity, and despite Diego Flores' general reputation as a sour and vindictive individual, his advice on this occasion could hardly be faulted since most of the other Armada ships were already streaming away in the direction of

Armada!

Prawle Point, and if the *San Martin* had tarried in the gathering gloom, half the fleet could have been missing by morning.

Even then, and contrary to Pedro de Valdes' assertions, the *Rosario* was by no means abandoned, orders having been given for a flotilla of pinnaces to stand by, as well as the *San Francisco*, second ship of the Andalusian squadron, and the *San Cristobal*, flagship of the Castilians. There was even a second attempt to get a hawser aboard, and to remove some of the crew, but a combination of heavy sea, foul weather and darkness thwarted the Spaniards yet again.

Thus Pedro de Valdes, writing from captivity in England, was nothing like as ill-served as he represented to King Philip. Why should he have claimed otherwise? Clearly he needed to place the best complexion possible upon his own conduct, and in this respect it is interesting to note that in his letter to the king he attributed the start of his troubles to a collision with a Biscayan, whereas it was with a ship from his own squadron, thus suggesting poor sailing discipline among the Andalusians.

Beyond that, whatever the state of relations between himself and Diego Flores, he had also crossed swords with Medina Sidonia while the Armada waited at Corunna. At a council-of-war, he had been all for pressing on despite some thirty missing ships and inadequate victualling, and so strongly had he argued in the face of more experienced colleagues that the normally controlled duke seems to have lost his temper. As a consequence, de Valdes had found it advisable to pen a hasty note to the king to put his version of events, just as he subsequently did over the loss of his ship.

To return, meantime, to the *Rosario* herself, wallowing helplessly in steep seas, with her potential rescuers standing helplessly by. The picture of what happened next is supplied by a petition submitted to Lord Howard by the officers of the *Margaret and John*, 200-ton privateer, of London. This petition sought to establish a claim to part of the booty from de Valdes' ship, and therefore it may carry an element of exaggeration, but the basic facts are probably accurate enough.

According to the petition, the *Margaret and John* sped up to the *Rosario* quite alone, having outstripped the rest of the English fleet, upon which the Spanish ships, standing by, hastily took themselves off.

After a wary look at the stricken ship, the London boat came hard under her sides, but she was a tall and forbidding vessel, probably three or more times the size of the greyhound of an English ship, and so 'by reason of her greatness, and the sea being very much grown, we could not lay aboard without spoiling our own ship. And, therefore, seeing not one man show himself, nor any light appearing in her, we imagined that most of her people had been taken out, and to try whether any were aboard or not, we discharged 25 or 30 muskets into her cagework, at one volley. And presently they gave us two great shot, whereupon we let fly our broadside through her ...'

A lonely and frightening night it must have been for the crew of the now deserted *Rosario*, realizing as they would have done that if the cruel sea did not spell their end, then long and miserable captivity was the best that all but a few could expect.

So far as can be judged, no other ship attacked the Spaniard that night, although de Valdes' letter to the king reported, perhaps typically, that he was forced to defend himself till daylight. As for the *Margaret and John*, she left around midnight, as the English once more took up the pursuit of the Armada, her crew puzzling over the voice they heard calling from time to time in Spanish from the vicinity of the *Rosario*. Thinking maybe the voice came from a swimmer they had put out a boat, but had found nothing.

As for England's Lord Admiral, with the ships from Plymouth now joined, and with new men and fresh victuals sent out by John Hawkins' brother, who was mayor of that city, he could now confront the Spaniards once more in the encouraging knowledge that fortune had smiled on him that day and a valuable Armada feather or two had been plucked.

9 The Battle of Portland Bill

By dawn next day the Spanish fleet had progressed as far as Berry Head, the south-eastern extremity of Tor Bay, with Lord

Howard's flagship barely a cannon shot distant. But as the darkness lifted, the Lord Admiral made a disturbing discovery, only two other ships, the *Bear* and the *Mary Rose* were with him, the rest of his fleet seemed to have disappeared. With the light strengthening, the topmen aboard the *Ark* could eventually make out a scattering of English vessels half-mast high on the western horizon, but the number was nowhere near the full complement – something had clearly gone very wrong during the night.

Something had indeed gone wrong, and it was lucky for Lord Howard that the Armada did not seek to take advantage of it and attack his isolated detachment of ships.

The man responsible for the Lord Admiral's alarming predicament was none other than his principal lieutenant, the Vice-Admiral of the Fleet, Sir Francis Drake. His conduct that night, even if one gives him the benefit of the doubt and accepts that it was well intentioned, seems to have been highly irresponsible.

When the English ships had resumed their pursuit of the Armada late the previous evening, Lord Howard, probably in recognition of Drake's exploits during that day of skirmishes, had assigned to him the honour of leading the fleet, and so the poop lantern of the *Revenge* burned as a beacon for the procession of following vessels. At some time in the darkest part of the night, however, the *Revenge*'s light suddenly disappeared, to be seen no more. The result was confusion, for while the Lord Admiral's flagship sailed on, only the *Bear* and *Mary Rose* followed, other ships, bearing in mind their orders to follow the *Revenge*, either hove to or shortened sail. Thus, by daylight, many miles of sea separated the *Ark* from the rearmost of the English vessels.

What happened during the night, or what Drake claimed to have happened, was that his ship sighted a small group of unidentified vessels heading west on the seaward side of the fleet, and, suspecting they might be Spaniards attempting to work to windward of the English, he had doused the *Revenge*'s light, and, accompanied only by the *Roebuck* from his squadron, and a couple of pinnaces, had gone to investigate.

The westward-bound ships proved to be no more than German merchantmen, according to Drake, but what threw suspicion upon the episode was that at its conclusion, either by considerable good fortune or cunning design, the tiny flotilla made a highly advantageous discovery.

The nature of that discovery was learned by the enterprising crew of the *Margaret and John* when, having reached Lord Howard's flagship post-haste to stake their claim for prize money after the action of the previous night against the crippled *Nuestro Senora del Rosario*, they were told that Pedro de Valdes' vessel had now been captured as a prize – by none other than Sir Francis Drake.

The response of the Lord Admiral is not recorded, but at least one of Drake's senior colleagues, the irascible Yorkshireman, Martin Frobisher, made no secret of his opinion. The redoubtable Frobisher, five years older than Sir Francis at the age of fifty-three, had been at sea for some forty years and had led three expeditions in search of the north-west passage, thus he stood in no state of deference to Drake, quite the reverse, in fact, to judge from his irate words concerning the *Rosario* affair.

The vice-admiral, he declared, had deliberately worked back to de Valdes' ship '– because he would have the spoil. He thinketh to cozen us of our shares of fifteen-thousand ducats; but we will have our shares, or I will make him spend the best blood in his belly.'

Whether or not Frobisher's strictures were justified, Drake's risky initiative suggests that his years of buccaneering had rendered him ill-prepared to serve as a key element in so large a unit as the navy now was. Perhaps it was as well that the Armada venture proved so short-lived, otherwise some similar display of individualism might have proved costly.

Aboard the *Rosario*, de Valdes had at first been inclined to offer resistance when called upon to surrender, but having discovered his adversary was the mighty Drake himself, honour was sufficiently satisfied to permit him to yield with good conscience. As a consequence he had the unexpected experience of seeing the rest of the Armada campaign from the *Revenge*, where he was a regular guest at Drake's table.

The *Rosario*, with 50,000 escudos aboard and a crew of 400, was taken to Dartmouth, the crew enduring years of miserable incarceration in West Country prisons.

De Valdes and a handful of senior officers for whom good ransoms were expected, or for whom Englishmen detained in Spain might be exchanged, were lodged in relative comfort in private homes. Thanks to Drake's influence, de Valdes was able to hunt, and to lead an active social life, although his detention lasted over three years and only ended upon payment of a ransom of £3,000, about £250,000 at today's rates.

One probable reason why the Armada left Lord Howard's isolated trio of ships unmolested off Berry Head was because the damage sustained by a number of ships in the previous day's encounter, particularly Juan Recalde's galleon, was such as to require a major reorganization of the Spanish battle formation.

The *San Juan de Portugal* had been so thoroughly mauled that there could be no question of her resuming her key position until repairs had been made, and thus the attention of the Armada's senior commanders had turned to a restructuring of the fleet. It was decided that Alonzo de Leyva would take charge of one single rearward squadron consisting of forty-three of the best ships in the fleet, and the Duke of Medina Sidonia would command a forward squadron.

Accordingly, new written instructions were carried to every ship by a flotilla of six pinnaces, each pinnace containing a senior army officer together with men from the provost marshal's unit, the policemen of the Armada. These instructions specified the new order of formation, and the police presence was presumably intended to emphasize the grim warning accompanying the order, namely that if any ship left her appointed place in the formation, 'without further stay they should hang the captain of the said ship.'

Around mid-morning, as the Spanish fleet re-formed, the *San Salvador* was reported to be sinking as a result of the damage she had received the previous day when her magazine blew up, so the order was given for her to be scuttled. For some unknown reason this was not carried out, but with no crew aboard, she slowly drifted away from the rest of the Armada, so that eventually, Lord Howard was able to despatch John Hawkins and Lord Thomas Howard to inspect the stricken vessel.

They were met by a sight of sickening desolation, with the Guipuzcoan's decks and steerage shattered, her stern blown out, and worst of all, the burnt bodies of some fifty men still aboard.

So foul was the stench and so ugly the sight that only the briefest inspection ensued before the two officers hastened off to the *Ark* to make their report, as the result of which, Captain

Thomas Fleming in the *Golden Hind* was instructed to get the *San Salvador* back to Weymouth, which was reached the next day.

Meanwhile the Armada made steadily eastwards in light breezes throughout that Monday, skirting Lyme Bay and seeing Portland Bill before them, while astern, the English gathered slowly into a compact force once more after the confusion of the previous night. By dusk, when Lord Howard's ships were again within range of their quarry, the wind had dropped completely so that eventually the two fleets lay motionless off the coast of Dorset. As the moon rose on this deceptively tranquil panorama, the Spanish could see that one group of English vessels had not, in the end, succeeded in closing with the rest of the navy, and lay distant and potentially vulnerable. It was an ideal opportunity for the Spaniards to attack, once the wind stirred again, and thus several of the Armada's most senior officers hastened to the flagship to urge such action.

Given the uncertainty about the direction of the next wind, it was clear that the four galleasses in the fleet would have a vital part to play in any attack, since their oarsmen could bring the quartet up to the isolated English ships and keep them engaged until the galleons arrived to grapple.

But it was typical of Medina Sidonia's luck that the previous day he had drawn the anger of the commander of the galleasses, Don Hugo de Moncada, by refusing his request to lead an assault on the *Ark* and the other two ships which had found themselves alone in the shadow of the Armada after Drake's pursuit of the German merchantmen. The ritual of warfare dictated that any attack on the commander of the English navy was the exclusive privilege of the Armada's commander, and so, possibly encouraged by his mentor, Diego Flores de Valdes, the duke declined to allow Moncada to usurp that privilege.

Now, however, the cooperation of Moncada was vital, and so the admiral of the Guipuzcoans, Miguel de Oquendo, was sent on a delicate diplomatic mission. According to Spanish accounts, Oquendo was empowered by Medina Sidonia to promise the offended Moncada the gift of an estate producing 3,000 ducats a year, in return for his participation in the proposed action. Tempting as that offer might have been, the wounded pride of this grandee, son of the Viceroy of Catalonia, was not to be so easily assuaged. Thus at dawn, when the attack was to have been launched, the galleasses were seen to be lying too far inshore to play an effective part.

On the face of things, this was an act of deliberate disobedience, and had Moncada not been killed a few days later, he might well have been eventually called to account.

The morning brought some consulation to Medina Sidonia, however, because the wind shifted to the north-east, so blowing for once in the Spaniard's favour. To gain the wind of an opponent, to have, in effect, first call upon this vital source of propulsion, was a basic tenet of sea warfare in the days of sail. To hold the wind, in other words, was to command the initiative, and so there now commenced an elaborate ballet, gradually progressing to battle, as the English strove to get the wind of the Armada.

It must have been a fascinating spectacle that morning off Portland Bill, with up to 200 ships heeling and tacking across miles of water as each navy sought to outsail the other, with the mariners sweating at their creaking tackle and the soldiers grouped tensely on deck awaiting the first shots of combat.

With their more nimble ships, and preponderance of seamen over soldiers, it was always likely that the English would gain the upper hand, but that day's battle, which from historical sources is merely to be glimpsed in fragments, as if through the smoke of war, seems certainly to have been the most fluid, and probably the most furious, which either side can have experienced up to that moment.

For the Spanish, that wind shift to the north-east was something of an impediment to their central objective of proceeding to their juncture with the Duke of Parma, but at the same time it offered the tantalizing prospect of at last getting to close quarters with the enemy.

The English, on the other hand, needed the weather gauge above all else, and so soon after dawn, Lord Howard led his fleet towards the shore in an attempt to get round the landward flank of the Armada. But Medina Sidonia covered this move, standing away on the same tack with the rest of his ships strung out to the south-east, and thus, with his opening gambit checked, Howard cast about on a westward tack, making out to sea as if to weather the newly-created rearward squadron which Alonzo de Leyva commanded, but de Leyva would have none of that and, altering course, led his ships directly towards the English. Their line-abreast formation presented an inviting target to Lord

Howard's gunners, however, and soon broadside after broadside thudded into the Spaniards as a dozen or so Englishmen sped across the face of the advancing squadron in their now-familiar single file formation.

Howard had with him in that first sharp confrontation several of the most able captains in the fleet, including John Hawkins in the *Victory*, Sir Robert Southwell aboard the *Elizabeth Jonas*, and Thomas Fenner in the *Nonpareil*, while among the Spaniards, in addition to de Leyva in the *Rata Coronada*, ships from the Levant squadron were prominent, including the huge *Regazona*, the squadron flagship, commanded by Martin de Bertendona.

It was Bertendona's vessel which, in the face of intimidating gunfire, continued boldly on in an effort to board the English flagship, but Lord Howard was not to be caught like that and so led his ships away to leeward.

At the conclusion of this encounter the English had had slightly the worse of things because they had failed to get to windward of the Armada and were now considerably strung out, so much so, in fact, that Frobisher in the *Triumph*, together with half a dozen smaller vessels, found themselves cut off towards the shore.

The four galleasses were closest to these beleagured Englishmen, but possibly still angry about his snub of the previous day, Hugo de Moncada was showing little inclination to lead his squadron into the attack. Soon, however, Medina Sidonia brought the *San Martin* alongside him, his temper clearly roused by Moncada's inactivity. In the euphemistic words of a Spanish observer, the duke bawled at the leader of the galleasses words which were understood to be 'the reverse of complimentary'.

The duke's own note of the encounter strikes a lower key, merely stating that his instructions were 'that by oar and sail they should endeavour to close with the enemy', but there seems little doubt that his tongue-whipping was effective, because pretty soon Moncada was moving in to take over the initiative from the handful of smaller ships which were already engaged with the English.

For the space of one-and-a-half hours, according to Lord Howard's report, the giant *Triumph* and the smaller merchant ships which supported her, slugged it out with the Spaniards, neither side getting in a decisive blow.

Relief came at last for Frobisher when Lord Howard himself sailed into the conflict, supported by a number of the ships which had fought alongside him in the earlier encounter with de Leyva's squadron. Now the tempo of battle began to rise as the English moved to within little more than musket shot before discharging their cannon, and the Spaniards made repeated attempts to grapple.

Observing the course of this fight, Medina Sidonia headed towards it with sixteen of the Armada's most powerful galleons, but even as the English braced themselves for this new assault they saw all but the *San Martin* break away and head out to sea once more. The reason was that as on the first day of battle, Juan de Recalde in the *San Juan* was cut off and under attack from a dozen English ships.

Meanwhile the *San Martin* held her course, and as she drew near to the *Ark*, Medina Sidonia ordered her topsails lowered and turned her broadside on to the English flagship. According to the rules, Lord Howard should have accepted the challenge at that point and gone alongside to allow the troops aboard the two vessels to test their skill in hand-to-hand combat. But the Spaniards had still not grasped the fact that the rules had been rewritten, war at sea was now a different game, so that instead of tilting at his opponent like some medieval knight, the English admiral, to the undoubted disgust of the Spaniards, merely discharged a broadside at the inviting target which the Armada flagship presented then sailed unchivalrously on while the following ships of his group did the same.

During this time the wind had begun to change, from north-east to south-east and eventually to south-west, which meant that despite several unsuccessful attempts to gain the wind during the day's fighting, it was now presented to the English by the grace of nature.

With the wind shifting thus, another furious battle began to develop further from the shore as an English force of some fifty ships, probably led by Francis Drake, attacked the seaward wing of the Armada. Shrouded as much of this action was, even from the participants themselves, by the heavy clouds of gunsmoke which hung over the water, it is not surprising that no clear picture emerges of its pattern.

What is well attested, however, is the progress of the fight into which Medina Sidonia had plunged his flagship. For an hour and more the *San Martin* withstood the English alone, Lord Howard's squadron receiving additional support as ships which had been attacking Recalde joined him. Shot after shot pounded into the hull of the Spanish flagship and flew around the super-structure. Rigging was torn, spars shattered and the sacred Armada standard cut in two, but she was a sturdy ship, double-timbered in good Spanish oak, and despite being holed, could soak up the punishment. Meantime, her own guns were worked to such good effect that before long, all but the boldest English ships were firing at the limit of their range to avoid being hit themselves.

Eventually relief came for the *San Martin* as other Spaniards arrived, the newly-combined force making its way to the east as most of the Armada, its formation broken by the whirl of conflict, streamed on ahead. In the words of Lord Howard, '– after wonderful sharp conflict, the Spaniards were forced to give way and flock together like sheep', but what the Lord Admiral did not mention was that the Armada was still on course for its ren-dezvous with the Duke of Parma.

The battle had lasted twelve hours, and been fought in its disjointed way over many leagues of Channel water. If that day, 2 August 1588, had not been the most decisive in naval warfare it had almost certainly been the noisiest to date as gunfire roared virtually nonstop. In words which may be attributed to Lord Howard himself, '– there was never seen a more terrible value of great shot, nor more hot fight than this was.'

And yet, and yet, for all that day of sound and fury, for all that 'terrible value of great shot', not a single Spanish vessel had been sunk and the Armada was re-forming.

Although the English again held the weather gauge, the Armada would not have been too much disconcerted by the events of the day.

10 *Commanders' Concerns*

When London learned of the Armada's arrival there was a rush of young bloods eager to join the fray. Everyone made for Portsmouth, looking for a ship, even the not-so-young Sir Horatio Palavicino, Genoese by birth but now one of Queen Elizabeth's principal bankers, even Sir Horatio set off for Portsmouth, fired by the zeal which burned in every man of spirit.

Another who dashed away was Lord Howard's twenty-eight-year-old brother-in-law, Robert Cary. He rode post-haste in the company of the Earl of Cumberland on the day of the Portland battle, and boarded a frigate the next morning. All that day, and on through the night, they searched for the English fleet, finally locating it at dawn – at least, they thought it was the English fleet. With the frigate almost in amongst the assembled ships it suddenly tacked frantically away – it was the Armada they were trying to join!

When the English ships were eventually discovered, Robert Cary boarded the flagship, but soon found that a lot of other young bucks had had the same idea, and so transferred to the *Elizabeth Bonaventure*, the vessel which had been Francis Drake's flagship the year before, when his squadron had, in his own words, 'singed the King of Spain's beard'.

In view of his relationship to the Lord Admiral, it was natural that Cary should first make for the *Ark Raleigh*, or the *Ark Royal*, as it had now been renamed, because Lord Howard had already ensured that his family was well represented in the fleet, and would doubtless have welcomed another member.

The most senior Howard after the Lord Admiral himself was his nephew, Lord Henry Seymour, commander of the squadron guarding the Narrow Seas, the stretch of water between Dover and Calais. Three other relatives also commanded ships, all in Howard's squadron, and two more were serving aboard the *Ark*.

The fact that none of them had much sea experience, and that nepotism had placed them where they were, caused no one any particular concern or surprise. It was an accepted fact that the well-born should command, and it was also accepted that the Lord Admiral would place as many of his family as possible in responsible positions – at least he could hope to rely on them for their personal allegiance.

All the same, it was lucky for England that alongside these aristocratic tyros sailed commoners of the calibre of Drake, Hawkins, Frobisher and half-a-dozen others. The Spanish could boast nothing like the same depth of skill and experience among their captains.

If the Armada was an exciting challenge to the young nobility and their boon companions, there was a good deal of alarm among the less exalted, who could only sit at home, waiting and worrying. Despite all the stern warnings from the Government, the extensive preparations, the additional taxes, somehow, many an Englishman had never been convinced that the Spaniards would actually come, but now that gunfire was to be heard in the Channel, and those dire rumours about cruel Spanish intentions were recalled, the atmosphere grew heavy with foreboding. And thus, throughout the land, churches were packed as people prostrated themselves in prayer and supplication, none more fervent in their prayers than those Protestants whom the Spaniards had threatened by name.

As the churches filled, so the militia began to muster, thus causing Lord Burghley more agonizing as to how everything was to be paid for. Only when militiamen were actually called to the Crown's service did they come on to the government's payroll, at all other times their charges were met by local levies, but now that critical time had come.

'I shall but fill my letter with more melancholy matter,' Burghley wrote at the conclusion of a note to Walsingham concerning the State's precarious finances, 'if I should remember what money must be had to pay 5,000 footmen and 1,000 horsemen for defence of the enemy landing in Essex.'

Those troops were assembling at Tilbury, where a few days later Queen Elizabeth was to score what today would be called a magnificent public relations triumph, as she sought to rally her forces in the nation's hour of peril.

The gathering militiamen were the responsibility of the Earl of

Leicester, the queen's old favourite and now commander of the land forces. But Leicester was not a born general, his handling of the English army sent to the Netherlands in 1584 after the assassination of the Prince of Orange had been undistinguished, to say the least, and to judge from his correspondence, the burden of high command had become all too stressful by the time of the Armada.

This stress was manifesting itself in a continuous series of complaints to Walsingham; the earl was angry, for example, that he had not been officially informed about the disabling of those two Armada ships off the coast of Devon in the first day's fighting, but had merely heard of it 'as news commonly spread abroad'. He was furious with his deputy, Sir John Norris, for staying too long with the troops guarding Dover, thus forcing Leicester to 'cook, cater, hunt' at Tilbury, in other words, to do everything single-handed. He was annoyed that some militia captains had marched their men to the camp with 'not so much as one meal's provision of victual', and he was worried that despite advertising for victuallers two days before setting up the Tilbury camp, not one had turned up.

He was concerned, too, that it was going to take five days just to gather a significant militia force from the immediate neighbourhood, so 'what will it be, and must be, to look in short space for those that dwell, 40, 50 and 60 miles off?'

(So much for Lord Burghley's boast to Spain's ambassador in Paris that a force of 20,000 English troops could be assembled in forty-eight hours!)

Finally, the noble Leicester was almost choleric over the navy's seemingly insatiable demands for men and ammunition, demands which had 'put me to more travail than ever I was in before.' It was Lord Henry Seymour from whom the latest call had come, but, expostulated Leicester, 'Good Lord, how is this come to pass, that both he and my Lord Admiral is so weakened by their men? I hear their men to be run away, which must be severely punished, or else all soldiers will be bold.'

It was a good thing the Spaniards never invaded, because added to the doubts about the militia's efficiency must have been larger doubts both about their commander's ability and state of mind. As his letters showed, this less-than-adequate general was almost at the end of his tether as he prepared at Tilbury; within a month, at the age of fifty-eight, he was dead.

The night before the battle off Portland Bill, the Duke of Medina Sidonia had despatched another messenger to the Duke of Parma in the hope of learning how matters stood with the troops in Flanders. There had been total silence following the launching of a previous emissary several days earlier, and the situation was becoming extremely worrying.

Perhaps Parma himself was feeling aggrieved since he had at one time been as much in the dark about the Armada's preparations as Medina Sidonia continued to be about his. The general had sent a representative, Captain Francisco Morisini, to Lisbon in early May to find out what was going on, but having learned everything, Morisini had been considered too great a security risk to be allowed to return alone in case the English caught him on the way back. So he was made to wait and sail with the Armada, only being sent back to Parma's headquarters in mid-June.

None the less, by the time of the Portland battle, not only Morisini but at least one other messenger from the Armada would have reached the general's camp, so that he was bound to have had a much clearer impression of events than the hapless Duke of Medina Sidonia. For not only did the duke lack the slightest scrap of information about the readiness or otherwise of the Flanders force, he also lacked a much more fundamental piece of information, namely, where his great force of ships might find refuge in an emergency.

What he wanted, he told Parma, were pilots who knew the coast of Flanders, 'as without them I am ignorant of the places where I can find shelter for ships as large as these, in case I should be overtaken by the slightest storm.'

It was an acutely uncomfortable predicament for the Armada's commander, but the trouble was that Parma was also short of pilots familiar with that coastline, the rebellious Dutch having forbidden any of their men to assist him. And although seamen were recruited from Italy and Germany, there were not enough of them, and they were unfamiliar with the treacherous coast of Flanders.

If Medina Sidonia was worried about pilots, Parma was equally concerned about what he saw as a basic misconception held by the former, a misconception about which the king had been made aware several months earlier, but seemed to have done nothing to clarify. This was the fact that the Armada commander was under the mistaken impression that the Flanders force was equipped with ships large enough and powerful enough to sail out into the Channel and reinforce his fleet once it arrived at the point of rendezvous.

That, in fact, was out of the question, Parma had stressed to King Philip, 'Most of our boats are only built for the rivers, and they are unable to weather the least sea. It is quite as much as they can do to carry over the men in fair weather, but as for fighting as well, it is evident they cannot do it, however good the troops in them may be.'

If an aspect as elementary as that was left uncorrected, how many other flaws in the enterprise might have come to light had the invasion of England actually been attempted?

Although Parma's enthusiasm for the venture seems to have declined with the dramatic decline in the strength of his troops, he had, nevertheless, made extensive preparations over many months, and it remains a mystery, therefore, why he was so patently unready when the Armada arrived.

Ideally, his fleet of landing craft would have been launched from some Zeeland port such as Flushing, but a force of Dutch ships under the command of Count Justin of Nassau controlled that area, so that it had been necessary for Parma to make complicated and expensive alternative arrangements. To enable his flotillas of flat-bottomed boats to reach the ports of Dunkirk and Nieuport, from which they were to embark, he had employed several thousand labourers in the task of cutting a series of canals across Flanders from places such as Ghent and Bruges.

The craft themselves had been commandeered from far and wide, in addition to which, Parma had also had several hundred barges built, each capable of carrying up to thirty horses.

Portable bridges had been made, too, from a store of some 20,000 barrels, and specially designed contrivances of beams and pikes had been manufactured, intended for blocking up harbours and inlets.

The troops themselves were to be supplied with bundles of faggots, behind which they could find some flimsy protection after landing on English beaches. They had also received frequent embarkation practice, Parma reported to the king, and could be at sea in quick time, despite the dearth of seamen. But it was impossible to keep the men in the boats for any length of time owing to the small size and primitive nature of the craft. 'There is no room to turn round,' he told the monarch, 'and they would certainly fall ill, rot and die.'

That army of his, a polyglot assembly of Spaniards, Italians, Walloons, Burgundians, Dutch, German, Scots and a handful of English, had become over the years virtually an autonomous force, a force too threatening for King Philip ever to allow it to return to Spain. But the Armada's slow preparation had been a time of real trial for Parma and his men, with thousands dying in the preceding winter of cold and damp, and the rest eking out a thoroughly miserable existence owing to the chronic shortage of money from which the army was suffering. During those early months of 1588, the duke had scooped the very bottom of the moneylenders' barrel in Antwerp, descending from borrowing at exorbitant rates of interest to eventually being able to raise no loans at all.

It was hardly surprising, therefore, that during that apparently endless wait for Medina Sidonia's ships to appear, there should rumble among that Flanders force the constant threat of mutiny.

11 *The Isle of Wight Battle*

The morning after the Portland battle, as the frigate carrying Robert Cary and the Earl of Cumberland left Portsmouth and began its search for the English fleet, and as the first news of the Armada was being learned in the Midland shires, Lord Howard's main concern was to get his exhausted stock of powder and shot replenished. Thus for several hours a continuous procession of barques and pinnaces plied between ships and shore as armouries all along the South Coast were denuded of their contents. The Lord Admiral also received the ammunition captured aboard Pedro de Valdes' crippled galleon, another useful contribution.

Prior to this resupply operation, soon after dawn, a brisk action had developed between the leading English ships and the flagship of the cargo boats, the *Gran Grifon*, which had got herself cut off. The fight cost the flagship some seventy dead and as many wounded, and for a while seemed likely to boil up into something much bigger, but when the English saw Medina Sidonia's squadron preparing to join in, they broke off the action.

The fact was that at that moment Lord Howard's ships needed a breather; not only were they low on powder and shot but the fighting of the previous day had shown them to be weak on tactics and this needed urgent consideration. A flag of council was accordingly displayed from the *Ark*, summoning the fleet's principal officers to confer.

In the confusion of that day-long battle, opportunities had gone begging, and precious ammunition had been wasted, simply because the English fleet lacked any effective organization. The new style of attack was a novel experience for everyone, its fluid, broken pattern perhaps more akin to an aerial dogfight than to the slow, formal manoeuvres of previous sea battles, but although the speed and dexterity of the English ships had constantly troubled the Spaniards, these qualities had been nullified by the lack of coordinated tactics.

For most of the time since its appearance in the Channel, the Armada had displayed an organization and discipline which seemed to render it almost impregnable, a factor the more noteworthy because of the need not merely to withstand English attacks but constantly to protect the vulnerable cargo vessels.

It was a major challenge to the tacticians in Lord Howard's fleet.

The solution which emerged from that council aboard the *Ark* was to divide the navy into four squadrons, the aim being to launch coordinated attacks from four different points in order to break the Armada's formation and so hinder its relentless eastward progress.

Three of the squadrons were to be commanded, predictably, by Lord Howard, Drake and Hawkins, while the fourth was given to Frobisher, probably because of the resolution he had displayed under fire the previous day.

And so, in its new formation, with each of the four squadrons containing both royal ships and merchantmen, the English fleet once more set off in pursuit of the Spaniards, whose lofty assembly of vessels appeared to some among Lord Howard's fleet almost too vast in weight for the sea to support.

But this was not the only aspect of superiority the Armada seemed to hold – consider that soaring cavalcade of saints and martyrs represented by King Philip's ships and compare their names with those borne by the English vessels. Set the Biscay ship, *La Concepcion de Zubelzu*, alongside the *Bark Buggins*, serving with Sir Francis Drake; *Nuestra Senora del Barrio*, from the Castilians, and the *Pansy*, from the port of London. Consider the saintly Portuguese squadron of royal ships, *San Marcos, San Felipe, San Luis, San Mateo*, and the prosaically named *Violet, Makeshift, Moonshine* and *Toby* from the English fleet.

But what's in a name? Certainly nothing to deter men who knew the sea as well as Drake, Hawkins and that supporting retinue of captains who served their nation so ably at this time, nothing to deflect their pursuit of the Armada as it headed towards its proposed anchorage off the Isle of Wight.

It was there, the council-of-war aboard the *San Martin* had agreed several days earlier, the fleet would wait until news arrived from the Duke of Parma, so in that vicinity it duly paused as night fell.

To the English, this pause suggested the ominous possibility of an attack on the Isle of Wight; an attempt to seize one South Coast port or another had always been anticipated, now it seemed it was to happen.

When dawn came the next day, the feast day of St Dominic, patron saint of Medina Sidonia's family, the two navies lay motionless on a sea of dead calm – unfavourable conditions for Lord Howard's agile, weatherly ships. But when the growing light revealed a large Spanish galleon some way astern of the rest of the Armada, and a second isolated vessel nearby, John Hawkins ordered out boats and had the rowers tow the ships of his squadron to within range of the two Spaniards, so close, in fact, that the oarsmen came under musket fire and had to retreat quickly.

The bigger of the two vessels was the *San Luis*, from Medina Sidonia's squadron, the other, an Andalusian merchantman, the *Santa Anna*, and as they both came hotly under fire, the Armada commander ordered the galleasses to their rescue, the ranks of galley-slaves propelling their ships swiftly across the calm waters towards John Hawkins' squadron. Three of the four galleasses were involved, one towing de Leyva's *Rata Coronada* for added support, and for a while it seemed that the stationary English ships would be surrounded and overpowered.

Seeing the danger, Lord Howard had the *Ark* towed into the fray, and following him came his cousin, Lord Thomas Howard, in the *Golden Lion*. According to the English version of events, both the *Ark* and the *Lion* scored hits on the galleasses (there is no record of Hawkins' activities) so that one galleass limped away with a visible list, a second had her poop lantern shot away and the third sustained damage to her prow.

That minor encounter, which ended when a sudden wind enabled the beleagered Spanish ships to rejoin the Armada, was but the overture to another day of conflict, for with the rising wind the scene was all action once more, the mounting chorus of gunfire clearly audible to the militia forces waiting tensely in their hastily assembled camp on the Isle of Wight.

It was another of those Armada battles glimpsed imperfectly from the hasty records of a handful of the combatants, but one thing which emerges plainly is that, as in the Portland battle, Frobisher's *Triumph* was once again isolated and in danger of being boarded.

She had been standing inshore of the Armada with several other ships of Frobisher's squadron, positioned somewhere near the eastern approach to the Isle of Wight, when a fight developed with the *San Martin* and one of the galleasses. On the Spaniards' own admission, the opening stages of this fracas saw them getting the worst of things, with the English ships moving in closer than in previous battles, so that a number of soldiers aboard the *San Martin* were killed and her mainstay was severed.

For some reason, the rest of the Armada's vanguard had not followed when Medina Sidonia engaged Frobisher's ships, and now, with the new-found wind providing mobility, it was the Spanish rearguard which came charging to their commander's rescue. Seeing this large force bearing towards them, all the

English except the *Triumph* managed to slip away towards the remainder of the fleet, but Frobisher's vessel had been the most northerly of the squadron when the action began and, lacking the agility of the others, now found herself cut off.

The great size of the *Triumph* had convinced the Spaniards that she must be Lord Howard's flagship, and this lent added determination as half a dozen of the Armada's most powerful galleons bore down upon her. Situated as he was to leeward of the enemy, there was only once chance of escape for Frobisher and that was to try to tow out of danger. Accordingly his boats were hastily slung out and as the sweating oarsmen inched the cumbersome *Triumph* towards the windward station, her captain lowered his ensign and fired off three guns to signal his distress. This alert brought longboats from several other ships scudding across the water, and soon no fewer than eleven of them were towing her. Even so, the Spaniards, with the *San Martin* and the *San Juan*, Recalde's ship, in the van, were visibly gaining, and as he watched other vessels of Lord Howard's fleet laboriously toiling to the *Triumph*'s aid, it seemed certain to the Duke of Medina Sidonia that at last the opportunity was coming to board the English 'wherein was the only way to victory'.

He was not to have such luck, however, because even as Frobisher's closest protectors, the *Bear* and the *Elizabeth Jonas*, grimly awaited the Spanish onslaught, the wind suddenly veered in favour of the English, and with the *Triumph* hastily putting on sail and casting off the longboats, all three were able to slip beyond the Spaniards.

While this action was taking place towards the shore, another fight was developing on the Armada's seaward flank, the consequences of which could have been disastrous for it.

For some time the Spaniards had had the wind, so that the English, in the shape of the squadrons commanded by Drake and Hawkins, were forced to give way and for a time were in some trouble, as the master of one of the ships in the Andalusian squadron later described. 'We found the wind fair and were aweather of them, going very near and they flying,' he reported. 'We had them broken and the victory three parts won, when the enemy's *capitana* turned upon our Armada, and the galleon *San Mateo*, which had the point of the weather wing, gave way to it, retreating into the body of the Armada. Seeing that, the enemy took heart and turned with his whole fleet, or greater part of it, and charged upon the said wing in such wise as we who were there were driven into a corner ...'

Normally 'the point of the weather wing', i.e. the strategically important tip of the wing, was held by Recalde's ship, the fifty-gun *San Juan*, but since she was busy with the *Triumph*, her place had been taken by another of the royal Portuguese galleons, the smaller and less heavily armed *San Mateo*, carrying just thirty-four guns. She had clearly been surprised and disconcerted when an Englishman, probably Drake in the *Revenge*, suddenly and defiantly turned upon her, so that her confusion spread to other ships in that seaward wing. But the true significance of this English manoeuvre was not that it thwarted an anticipated Spanish victory but that it set the Armada on a course to potential disaster.

With English guns once more pounding their starboard flank, the Spaniards began edging away north-eastwards, and perhaps, as has been claimed by some historians, this was indeed a deliberate strategy on the part of Drake and Hawkins – for by driving Medina Sidonia's ships in that direction, they were shepherding them towards one of the most dangerous pieces of water in the entire Channel, an area of treacherous shallows and broken rocks known as the Owers.

Fortunately for the Armada, the danger was duly perceived, a gun boomed out from the flagship, more sail was shaken out, and the entire fleet altered course to the south-east. It was a close-run thing, though, another few minutes on the northeasterly bearing could have had the Spaniards in direst peril, so an anonymous observer in the Spanish fleet was not greatly overstating the matter when he wrote that just as Medina Sidonia had had victory over the *Triumph* denied him by a hair's breadth, only by the same measurement had the Armada escaped disaster off the Owers.

With the Spaniards moving away eastwards the English could feel moderately satisfied with their morning's work. The fighting had lasted for five hours, from dawn until ten, 'with so great expense of powder and bullet,' reported Sir George Carey, who heard the entire battle from his camp on the Isle of Wight, 'that during the said time the shot continued so thick together it might rather have been judged a skirmish with small shot on land than a fight with great shot on sea.'

As Carey's relieved militia garrison struck the camp they had maintained since the previous Monday, Lord Howard's fleet made no immediate attempt to pursue the Armada, most ships were low on ammunition once more, and were having to take aboard broken-up plough chains and other bits of scrap metal, since more shot was not to be had along that part of the coast. They would get to Dover, the Lord Admiral decided, rearming themselves there and at the same time linking up with Lord Henry Seymour's squadron from the Narrow Seas.

Just how successful they had been on this occasion could barely have been appreciated by even the most sanguine members of the fleet, because they were not to know how completely they had disrupted Spanish intentions. Not only had they eliminated the threat to the Isle of Wight, a victory in itself, but they had driven the Armada well beyond the point where Medina Sidonia and his colleagues had agreed to wait for news from the Duke of Parma. Instead of waiting, the Spaniards were now heading, *faute de mieux*, towards the point where they hoped to rendezvous with him, forced to sail on without the slightest knowledge of Parma's situation, or, for that matter, where that great assemblage of ships might safely settle itself if the general required it to pause.

It must have been with a particular sense of urgency, therefore, that the Armada's commander despatched another messenger to Parma's headquarters as his fleet put the Isle of Wight and the English fleet well astern. The message Captain Pedro de Leon carried informed him 'that he should come out with as little delay as possible to join with this fleet.'

It was another wasted journey.

12 Anchorage at Calais

After five days of continuous contact, with only a couple of Spanish ships disabled and not a single one sunk, there were signs that morale in the English fleet was beginning to sag. The

Armada was proving far more formidable than most had imagined, proceeding as it did with a kind of brute determination which nothing seemed to deter.

Lord Howard clearly sensed the frustration which was starting to appear, and decided that a psychological boost was necessary. Accordingly, at a ceremony aboard the *Ark* on Friday, 5 August, six of his senior officers were knighted, among them John Hawkins, Martin Frobisher and two of the Lord Admiral's own kinsmen.

It was done, Howard related, 'in reward of their good services in these former fights, as also for the encouragement of the rest', and it was certainly a shrewd and well-timed gesture.

But if seeds of doubt were beginning to appear in the navy itself, the nation's enthusiastic support for the fleet remained strong; so numerous had the flow of volunteers now become, in fact, that boatloads were having to be turned away. Powder, shot, victuals and ships were all also being despatched as the navy made its way eastwards, so that, despite its failure to get in a visibly telling blow, its commander's situation was infinitely preferable to that of the increasingly worried Duke of Medina Sidonia.

The Duke of Parma's total silence was threatening to turn the enterprise into a fiasco, as well as endangering the lives of every one of the 30,000 men aboard those Spanish ships. A full week earlier the Armada's commander had sent off his first messenger, Don Rodrigo Tello, just at the time the Lizard was sighted, and another had been despatched from half-way up the Channel, but not a word had yet come from either.

Shortly after the Isle of Wight battle, Captain Pedro de Leon had set off for Dunkirk, but by the following day, Medina Sidonia had decided that still another reminder was necessary. The mission of Domingo Ochoa was not only to seek new supplies of shot, of which the Armada was now growing ominously short, but to stress once more the need for Parma to emerge with his sea-borne army as soon as the Spanish fleet came within sight off Dunkirk. The messenger was also to demand that flyboats be despatched to aid the fleet; forty flyboats had been the requirement, Medina Sidonia reported to King Philip, 'to the end he might be able with them to close with the enemy, because our ships being very heavy in comparison with the lightness of those of the enemy, it was impossible to come to hand-stroke with them.'

This was precisely the demand, which, months earlier, Parma had warned the king he would not be able to meet since he did not possess any flyboats. Such small, swift craft would have carried enough guns to have at least made themselves a nuisance to the English, but Parma's warning had obviously never been passed on by King Philip. Was this because the monarch felt that, in view of the divine nature of the venture, God would somehow provide a solution and that no human intervention was necessary, or was it that Parma did, in fact, possess such boats and the king knew it?

Certainly the English seemed to know the true position, to judge from the report which Lord Henry Seymour submitted to Walsingham. Seymour's squadron had been watching the ports of Dunkirk and Nieuport for several months, and so he was able to state that, among other craft, Parma's fleet included '40 sails of flyboats'.

Perhaps the explanation was that although the boats existed, they were neither adequately crewed nor armed for anything more than escort duty, although in the light of subsequent events this matter seems to add one more question mark against Parma's true attitude to the Armada enterprise.

There was no contact between the two fleets this day, with the Spaniards bearing in the direction of Calais, and, in Lord Howard's words, 'always before the English army like sheep'. The Lord Admiral was fond of this simile, and probably at that time, when Tudor England's wealth was drawn from the backs of the vast flocks of sheep which flourished there, that bunched mass of slow-moving, white-sailed Armada ships did indeed bring sheep at once to mind.

Apart from the ceremony of knighthood aboard the *Ark*, there was one other event of note for the English that day, when a French ship out of Le Havre was stopped and its crew questioned. From them, Lord Howard learned news to ease the mind of every man in his fleet – France was showing no signs of entering the conflict on the side of Spain. This was a fear which had long gripped Queen Elizabeth and her ministers; with French ports at its disposal, with French supplies of victuals and possibly of men, the Armada could linger in the Channel for weeks on end, choosing its own time to strike. Furthermore, if the French also put a fleet to sea, Lord Howard's force might be attacked simultaneously from front and rear. With the news from those Le Havre fishermen, such fears could be put aside.

The English also heard from the Frenchmen, doubtless with amused scorn, about the rumours starting to fly around Europe concerning the great victories already won by the Armada. One such rumour even had Queen Elizabeth captured and on her way to Rome, where she was to appear, a barefoot penitent, before Pope Sixtus.

Through a stormy Friday night and on into the next day, Lord Howard's ships dogged the Armada, the two fleets very close at times, but exchanging no shots, the Spaniards sailing in tight and ordered formation.

Around ten in the morning the coast of France came into view, in the vicinity of Boulogne, and for the next few hours the Armada beat north-eastwards, round Cap Gris Nez and on towards Calais.

'There were divers opinions as to whether we would anchor there or go on further;' Medina Sidonia reported, 'but the Duke, understanding from the pilots who were with him that, if he went further, the currents would carry him out of the English Channel and into the North Sea, he resolved to anchor off Calais, seven leagues from Dunkirk, from whence the Duke of Parma could join with him.'

The first the English knew of this decision was when, around 5 p.m., the anchors of every ship in the Armada went rumbling down, almost simultaneously it seemed, and the entire company of ships came to an abrupt stop. With a southwesterly wind behind Lord Howard's vessels, and a flood tide running, they might easily have been swept on past the Armada at that moment, and so lost the weather station, and, indeed, it appeared to the English that that had been the Spanish intention when anchoring so abruptly. The ruse failed, however, and they came to rest still to leeward of their opponents.

Medina Sidonia had approached Calais with a leaden sense of foreboding concerning Parma's preparedness and he was soon to find his fears fully justified. Just in case some act of fate had conspired to keep every one of his messengers from reaching the general, he now sent off the most senior emissary to date, Secretary Arceo, to report both the Armada's position two leagues off Calais, and its position *vis-à-vis* the English, 'the enemy's fleet being on my flank and able to bombard me, whilst I am not in a position to do him much harm.' If Parma could not immediately come out with all his force, Arceo was instructed to stress, he should at least send the flyboats already requested.

In addition to the Secretary, a second messenger left the *San Martin* that evening, bound for an interview with the Governor of Calais. The mission of Captain Pedro de Heredia was to explain to the Governor, Monsieur de Gourdan, why the Armada was anchored so close to the French port, and to assure him that the Spaniards bore nothing but goodwill.

Heredia returned some time later with the reassuring news that M. de Gourdan had warmly reciprocated the good wishes of the duke and, on behalf of the King of France, offered whatever services could be provided.

It was a small crumb of comfort, and it came at a moment when Medina Sidonia would have sorely needed it, because a little earlier he had watched, along with the rest of the Armada, as a new squadron of thirty-six ships arrived to join the English fleet. To the Spaniards, fatalistically observing this major rein-forcement of the enemy, that new squadron could mean only one thing, 'Juan Acines', almost as feared as the dreaded 'El Draque', had arrived. In fact, of course, John Hawkins had been with the English fleet from the first cannon shot, and the new ships were those of Lord Henry Seymour, but that name meant nothing in the Armada.

Seymour's squadron had had a boring, drudging time as the invasion threat mounted, patrolling for weeks on end on and off the coast of Flanders in summer weather as foul as any to be met in mid-winter, ever watchful for the Duke of Parma but seeing nothing. It was a particularly frustrating assignment since, as everybody knew, sooner or later those ships with Lord Howard away to the west would be in the thick of things if the Spaniards came, there would be action, excitement, and perhaps even a prize or two.

Even when a message arrived from Sir Francis Drake, reporting the first skirmishes against the Armada, Seymour's ships were still required to maintain their station in the Narrow Seas.

'I am most glad of this most happy beginning of victory obtained of her Majesty's enemies,' Lord Henry wrote to Sir Francis Walsingham, 'but most sorry I am so tied I cannot be an actor in the play.'

Now, at last, he was to have his hour upon the stage, although at its conclusion he was to be left just about as frustrated as during those long weeks of waiting.

The Armada's pause at Calais was a welcome relief for many aboard, not least those among the nobility and gentry who took the opportunity to stretch their legs ashore. It was welcome too to the good burghers of Calais, who swarmed aboard the anchored ships in large numbers, and even more welcome to the merchants of the port. For a prosperous twenty-four hours, just about every edible item which could be found was sold to the Spaniards, with eggs, in particular, rocketing to unheard of prices.

The temporary halt brought scant relief to the Armada's commander, however, because at dawn the following day, Sunday 7 August, the messenger he had despatched nine days earlier off the Lizard, Captain Rodrigo Tello, finally reported back. He bore the kind of tidings which the duke had probably steeled himself to expect, but which none the less much increased his troubles. Tello reported that although he had successfully reached Bruges, where the Duke of Parma's headquarters were then located, and informed him of the fleet's progress, the news appeared to have had little effect because at Dunkirk the previous evening the duke had not arrived, and neither men nor ammunition were aboard the waiting landing craft there.

Disturbing as this information was, it assumed much greater significance within an hour or so, when a nephew of the Governor of Calais arrived aboard the *San Martin* to warn Medina Sidonia that the Armada was anchored in an area of treacherous currents, and should urgently seek less dangerous moorings. Since Parma had completely failed to answer his earlier request concerning a safe haven for the fleet, the duke's dilemma was now painful.

Thus, no less a figure than the Inspector General of the Armada, Don Jorge Manrique, set off to Parma's headquarters to urge him to rapid action before the spring tides ended, and to find a port for the threatened ships. It was impossible to continue cruising with the fleet while waiting for the Flanders troops, Medina Sidonia stressed, 'as its great weight causes it to be always to the leeward of the enemy, and it is impossible to do any damage to him, hard as we might try'.

When Manrique finally found Parma he spoke so scathingly about the latter's unreadiness that a violent quarrel blew up and

Parma was only restrained from attacking him by some of his staff officers.

Meanwhile, Captain Tello's report about the state of affairs at Dunkirk was soon confirmed by a message from Secretary Arceo. The general had still not reached the port, he stated, no munitions had been embarked, and, in truth, it was impossible to see how everything could be made ready within a fortnight!

As he digested this shattering information, Medina Sidonia must have conjectured on the rapidity with which the odds had lengthened against the Armada. In the space of a few hours, three specific blows had fallen, the need to find a safe anchorage when none was known, the horrifying unreadiness of Parma, and, as he could observe from his traditional position at the taffrail of the *San Martin*, the reinforcement of the enemy fleet which had brought its numbers well above those of his own.

Aboard that English fleet, where, in the eyes of one envious Andalusian skipper, some of the great ships were the best he had ever seen both in handling and guns, discussions were taking place about how best to tackle that tethered concourse of Spaniards. Old Sir William Wynter, second-in-command of Lord Henry Seymour's squadron and a mariner for more than fifty years, had no doubt about what to do – send in the fireships.

He had been advocating such action in Lord Howard's cabin when there had come a great commotion and they had hurried on deck to discover that the fast-flowing tide had tangled the giant *Bear* with three other ships and sent all four crashing into the *Ark*. Luckily that piece of poor seamanship did little serious damage, so there was nothing to distract the senior officers who assembled in the Lord Admiral's cabin for another council-of-war, the outcome of which was agreement that they would indeed send in the fireships, that same Sunday evening.

Throughout the Armada, meanwhile, the sense of foreboding mounted; all the previous night the Spaniards had ridden at anchor 'with the enemy half a league from us likewise anchored, being resolved to wait, since there was nothing else to be done, and with great presentiment of evil from those devilish people and their arts,' reported one of the *San Martin*'s complement. 'So too in a great watching we continued on Sunday, all day long.'

There was, however, one moment of diversion during that

anxious Sunday vigil, when at about four in the afternoon, an English pinnace was seen approaching the Armada. With the kind of mad bravado in which Englishmen have indulged at some time or other in just about every war the nation has ever fought, the pinnace made straight for the flagship and fired four times into her vast, double-timbered flank. It then went nimbly about and with no more harm than a cannon shot through the topsail, sailed impudently back to the English fleet.

Although the physical damage inflicted by this unknown attacker was minimal, the psychological impact was considerable. 'It was much noted,' a Spaniard recorded, 'for its daring impertinence, and more than ever, we saw how by the use of very good and very light ships, it was possible for them to come and go any way they pleased, the which we could not do.'

By nightfall on Sunday, when Arceo's devastating assessment of Parma's unreadiness had reached Medina Sidonia, Spanish morale was sagging so alarmingly that a rumour was deliberately circulated that the Flanders troops would sail to join the Armada the following day. But although spirits were raised by this information, the sense of impending danger remained very strong.

There had been sinister movements among the English fleet as dusk gathered, ships shifting formation, and later, in the darkness of a moonless night, the flickering of lights which told of unusual activity. To experienced seamen that meant one thing – fireships, and thus the duke deputed one of the ablest men aboard the *San Martin*, Captain Antonio Serrano, to take charge of a flotilla of pinnaces and tackle any fireship which might approach the Armada. The captain may have been a brave man, but something more than bravery was needed that night.

13   *The Deadly Fireships*

About midnight the tide turned and began to flow with increasing momentum, the tides in Calais Road, where the

Armada now sat, being the fiercest anywhere in the eastern part of the Channel. With their ships straining against their double anchors like tethered horses, the anxious Spaniards gathered on the high poop decks became aware of more glimmering lights in the English fleet, and then, out of the dark night a fire blazed, then another, and another, in no time, eight fires were to be counted, eight blazing vessels bearing towards the Armada, carried inexorably onwards by the ever-quickening tide and freshening wind.

As the English crewmen who guided those fiery missiles climbed into rowboats and pulled back towards Lord Howard's fleet, their job bravely and expertly done, the Spanish pinnaces under Captain Serrano's command moved in to intercept the oncoming vessels, but each had been well-packed with explosives, including primed guns, and as soon as the first white-hot weapon exploded in a gout of flame and showering sparks, one name was on every man's lips – Giambelli, the fiendish Giambelli!

Three years earlier, 1,000 of the best men in the Duke of Parma's army had been slaughtered at Antwerp by the devilish devices of the Italian engineer, Federico Giambelli. These were fireships so loaded with explosives that they became huge floating bombs – 'hellburners', was the name Parma's men gave them. In the Armada it had been rumoured that the Italian was now in England's pay, so that when those fireship guns began to explode, fear swept through the entire fleet.

Watching that mass of flame moving towards his ships, the Duke of Medina Sidonia was not to know that although Giambelli was indeed working for the English he was actually constructing a defensive boom in the Thames (it broke on the first flood tide) and had played no part in preparing the burning vessels. Nor could the duke know that they carried only modest amounts of explosives and had been hastily prepared for their task.

His expectation as they came on towards the Armada was that Serrano's pinnaces would cope with them, getting grappling irons aboard and towing them aside, and that should any get through, then vessels in their path would merely slip their cables and stand away until the tide had carried them by.

With that first explosion, however, all such ordered plans seemed to have been blown away, to escape was the thing, to escape in any way whatever. Thus while some ships, including the *San Martin*, did indeed slip their cables, others simply hacked through theirs and, leaving their anchors on the seabed, ran urgently before the wind.

It was a brilliant success for the English, the turning point of the entire campaign, for although not one Spanish vessel fell victim to the fireships, the Armada had been shifted so effectively from its rendezvous area that it was never able to return.

'Fortune so favoured them,' one of the *San Martin*'s officers was later to declare, 'that there grew from this piece of industry just what they counted on, for they dislodged us with eight vessels, an exploit which with one hundred and thirty they had not been able to do nor dared to attempt.'

Considering, though, that more than a hundred Armada ships had jockeyed to escape, in darkness and with a full tide flowing, it was little short of providential for the Spaniards that only one casualty ensued, even if that was a major one, the flagship of the galleasses, Don Hugo de Moncada's *San Lorenzo*. She broke her rudder on a Levanter's cable – the galleasses all had weak rudders – and then collided with another ship, so that when a windy dawn arrived, she was sighted well inshore, crabbing awkwardly along and with her mainmast damaged.

Pretty soon the rudderless giant had been beached, almost under the guns of Calais castle, her 400 galley-slaves unable to prevent her running ashore – or perhaps scenting the possibility of freedom, making little effort to do so. In any event, there she lay, with the tide ebbing from beneath her so that she settled with an ever-increasing list, her deck tilted towards the shore and her seaward guns pointing uselessly up to the clouded sky.

Reclining there, she was a tempting target, and she certainly tempted the English, no less a person than the Lord Admiral, in fact. At a council-of-war the previous day, the most experienced campaigners around the table, men like Drake and Hawkins, had stressed the need to attack, immediately and in strength, once the fireships had done their work, but when daybreak revealed the crippled *San Lorenzo*, Howard took his squadron towards her, rather than leading the fleet to where the Armada lay strung out in disarray to the north-east.

Superficially, at least, this was an action on a par with Drake's abandonment of the navy the night he pursued those mysterious German merchantmen and ended by claiming the *Rosario* as a prize, and perhaps it was the thought of the galleass as a prize which led Lord Howard to her. Not that he would necessarily have sought to benefit personally, but the chance to plunder a Spaniard would have given a considerable boost to the morale of his squadron after days of apparently fruitless combat.

As it happened, the *Ark* drew too much water to get into action in the shallows where the *San Lorenzo* lay, but her pinnace was sent off, along with another from the *Margaret and John*, the doughty little London merchantman who had had that midnight encounter with the *Rosario* a week earlier.

Impotent as she might be, pitched up at such an angle there before Calais, the galleass was none the less more difficult to board than if she had been upright, and for half-an-hour or so the two boatloads of Englishmen bobbed about beneath her steeply sloping side, optimistically exchanging musket fire with the Spanish troops who peered from the deck high above. In that unfavourable situation, with no shred of protection, the English soon began to take casualties, including Lord Howard's lieutenant, Amyas Preston, who was gravely wounded. But just when it seemed the Spaniards would defy every effort, Hugo de Moncada himself was hit, a musket ball struck him full in the forehead, and he dropped dead.

At that, according to Richard Tomson, who commanded the pinnace from the *Margaret and John*, the troops aboard the *San Lorenzo* 'leaped overboard by heaps on the other side, and fled with the shore, swimming and wading. Some escaped with being wet; some, and that very many, were drowned.'

As for those few with an inclination to fight on, seeing a growing shoal of small English boats pulling towards them, they soon tied handkerchiefs to a couple of rapiers to call for a truce, at which, with a good deal of difficulty, the attackers hauled themselves aboard.

As the English went about their joyful work of plunder there emerged from the crowds of Frenchmen who had watched the fight from the adjacent shore, a delegation from the governor of Calais. The previous day, as the curious citizens of the port had swarmed aboard the Armada ships, the governor had sent presents and messages of goodwill to the Duke of Medina

Sidonia, now, with one of the duke's best ships a wreck beneath his castle walls, M. de Gourdan found himself forced to treat with her captors.

Lieutenant Tomson it was who parleyed with the French emissaries, he being the only Englishman there able to speak their language, and it was agreed between them that while the English were entitled to the contents of the *San Lorenzo*, the vessel herself, and her guns, were the prizes of the French. The governor's men eventually departed in an apparent mood of goodwill, and thus it was a considerable shock when, soon afterwards, the guns of Calais castle opened fire, hurling shot uncomfortably close to the swarming English and causing them hastily to abandon their booty-hunting.

The explanation for this seeming French treachery was finally discovered by Tomson, and it carries echoes of that present-day pestilence, English football hooliganism.

When the governor's emissaries were leaving the galleass, he learned, 'some of our rude men, who make no account of friend or foe, fell to spoiling the Frenchmen, taking away their rings and jewels, as from enemies, whereupon (they) going ashore and complaining, all the bulwarks and ports were bent against us, and shot so vehemently that we received sundry shot dangerously through us.'

Throughout this episode, Lord Howard had lingered with his squadron in deeper water, possibly wishing to ensure Moncada's potentially troublesome ship was indeed no longer a threat. Whatever the precise motive for remaining there, the fact of his doing so meant that the rest of the English fleet was temporarily disadvantaged as the biggest battle of the entire campaign began to develop further up the Channel, and the chance of striking a truly telling blow was thus lost.

14   *The Last Conflict*

Daylight on the morning after the fireship raid had not only revealed to the Duke of Medina Sidonia the disturbing prospect of the crippled *San Lorenzo*, far inshore, but the equally alarming sight of the rest of the Armada straggling haphazardly all along the coast towards Dunkirk.

The *San Martin* herself had anchored again after standing clear of the fireships, and had fired one of her big guns to order the rest of the fleet to do the same, but with many ships having lost their anchors, and others intent on putting as much sea as possible between themselves and the English, only the *San Marcos* from the duke's own squadron, together with a couple of smaller vessels, were near the flagship at daybreak.

With the wind from the south-west and the main body of the Armada lying well to leeward of Calais Road, there was no chance of the Spaniards regaining their former moorings, and so the *San Martin* weighed anchor and, followed by the *San Marcos* and the other two, bore north-eastwards to join with them.

As the English, minus Lord Howard's squadron, set off in pursuit, the pilots aboard Medina Sidonia's ship were coming to realize that if he tried to regroup the fleet in its present location, the whole concourse was liable to run aground on the Dunkirk banks. With insufficient sea-room, the scattered Spaniards needed time to work into deeper water, and the only way to gain time was for the most westward ships, the *San Martin* and her consorts, to hinder the approaching English. Thus the small flotilla went about to await the enemy charge, the duke meanwhile sending pinnaces off to order all the other vessels to sail as close to the wind as possible to avoid being driven on to the treacherous banks.

Given the speed and manoeuvrability of modern warships, there is something almost dream-like about battles between sailing ships, the sparring for tactical advantage, silently and with agonizing slowness, the barely perceptible narrowing of distance between the combatants, the mounting tension as the first roar of cannon-fire is awaited. The prelude to this day of action, the fiercest and bloodiest of all, brought suspense to the sharpest pitch of refinement as both sides, mindful of dwindling ammunition, held their fire as long as they dared.

Sir Francis Drake's *Revenge* launched the English attack, driving towards Medina Sidonia's defiant knot of vessels until the gap separating her from the *San Martin* was well within shouting range. Then Drake's bow guns spoke, followed by a broadside from his starboard battery, before the ship heeled away from the answering fire of the *San Martin* and bore north-eastwards towards where the main force of Spaniards was beginning to re-form in deeper water. After the *Revenge* came Thomas Fenner, in the *Nonpareil*, followed by the remainder of Drake's squadron, each ship exchanging shots with the Armada flagship and her supporting vessels before bearing away in pursuit of their vice admiral.

This rapier-thrust from the leading English squadron was to be succeeded by the bludgeon blows of the next two squadrons as the ships under Hawkins and Frobisher moved in to slog away at point blank range. This now became a confrontation displaying the kind of brute, mindless force of a struggle between dinosaurs, and had naval gunnery not been in its earliest infancy, the two groups of ships must have knocked each other to pieces. As it was, although the Spaniards took some heavy blows, Medina Sidonia bravely and stubbornly maintained his tack, thus allowing the rest of the Armada precious time to regroup.

As he saw the scattered Spanish ships, some fifty or so, slowly gathering into their familiar battle formation, Francis Drake must have cursed the lack of strategic foresight displayed by Hawkins and Frobisher, not to mention the distant Lord Howard. Drake himself was later to be accused of cowardice by the prickly Frobisher for the manner in which he had moved swiftly away from the fracas with the *San Martin* once he had fired his broadside, but the vice admiral was almost certainly looking beyond this localized affray to that larger body of leeward Spanish vessels.

With only some thirty ships from his own squadron available,

Drake had insufficient strength to make the telling intervention he had presumably hoped for, but had those two other squadrons also been on hand, it is probable that the agile English could have seriously hampered the regrouping Spaniards by attacking isolated ships before they could find the safety of the group.

But the chance was lost, so that eventually the conditions of weather and tide, plus the efforts of the Spaniards themselves, allowed Medina Sidonia's windward handful of ships to reunite with the leeward force and to take up their positions in the battle formation. Thereafter, like some ever-mounting fire, a mighty conflict developed, the rolling smoke of countless guns at times almost completely obscuring the two fleets, the carnage aboard some Spanish ships horrendous, their decks awash with blood as the hapless troops positioned there were scythed down.

All through this day-long battle, which bears the name of Gravelines, the coastal town between Calais and Dunkirk off which it was fought, the Armada consistently maintained its defensive formation, resisting all temptation to attack.

'Our fleet had the wind throughout,' reported the Genoese banker, Sir Horatio Palavicino, who had succeeded in getting aboard a ship at Portsmouth, 'and gave always the occasion to the enemy to open out and fight, but they chose rather to be followed, and to bear away, than to permit the fight to become general.'

These were bitter tactics for many a proud Spaniard to stomach, and there seems little doubt that Medina Sidonia, and, more particularly, his adviser, Diego Flores de Valdes, were strongly criticized by some in the Armada. There were even reports that officers aboard the *San Martin* hurled insults at the duke to try to goad him to attack.

But he was prepared to wait, optimistically as it transpired, for a time and place of his own choosing to fight back, and frustrating as this might have been for his men, it meant that the fleet emerged from that day of furious fighting far more intact than it might otherwise have done.

'Their force is wonderful great and strong,' Lord Howard was to report to Sir Francis Walsingham at the end of that day, 'and yet we pluck their feathers by little and little.'

The tactics the English were forced to employ to pluck those feathers were described by Palavicino: 'It was not convenient to attack them thus together and in close order,' he reported, 'for that our ships being of smaller size would have much disadvantage, but in the continued assaults ... they made them to feel our ordnance; and if any ship was beaten out of their fleet, she was surrounded and suddenly separated from the rest.'

Thus one sees the English stalking the Spaniards, charging in from time to time to disrupt their defensive formation, trying to pick off any weakened straggler.

Two of the biggest galleons in Medina Sidonia's own squadron were lost in this manner. Having been mauled in the early stages of the battle, the *San Felipe* and the *San Mateo* were initially rescued and nursed back into the protective crescent by that pillar of the Armada, Vice-Admiral Juan de Recalde, but when the English renewed their attack, those two royal Portuguese were vulnerable as wounded deer before hungry lions.

Lord Henry Seymour's ships launched this assault, having only just joined the battle through being anchored so far westward overnight, and Seymour's second-in-command, Sir William Wynter, described what happened. It was the seaward wing of the Armada at which the Narrow Seas squadron aimed their fire, he reported, and once again there was the sight of Spanish ships becoming entangled with one another as they crowded together for protection. The English had sailed in to within 120 paces before opening fire, and as their shot found its targets, Spanish crewmen began to leap overboard to escape the slaughter. Meanwhile the two damaged Portuguese galleons started to drop astern.

The first the Armada's commander knew of this was when, from somewhere to the rear of his ship, the sound of musket fire rattled across the smoke-shrouded sea. From his lofty position at the taffrail all he could make out was that a group of English vessels which a few minutes earlier had been attacking the *San Martin* were now groping through the smoke to surround two isolated ships of his fleet. So close were they approaching that the embattled Spanish crewmen, their powder and shot virtually exhausted, were defending themselves with the only serviceable weapons left, their muskets.

A glimpse of the intensity of the fight at this stage is supplied by a Spanish friar aboard a vessel which for some time fought alongside the *San Felipe*. The friar's ship had been raked with shot the instant it came within reach of the English, so that eventually, he declared, 'I saw myself that day in such sore straits that it was a miracle of God that we escaped; for since the ships were so scattered and could not help one another, the enemy's galleons came together and charged us in such numbers that they gave us no time to draw breath.'

As soon as Medina Sidonia perceived the plight of those two detached Portuguese galleons he gave the order to cast about and, sorely damaged as his own ship now was, limped back to their defence. Aboard the *San Mateo*, her commander, Don Diego Pimentel, who led the crack Sicilian unit of the Spanish army, was displaying the kind of suicidal bravery for which the military élite of Spain were renowned, never momentarily contemplating surrender even though his ship's plight grew worse by the minute. In fact, despite tattered sails, torn rigging and a hull which was battered and leaking, *San Mateo* was still seeking to grapple with any English ship which came within range. At length, with the carnage at its zenith, one of Lord Howard's vessels drew close to the shattered galleon and, from the rigging above the smoke of battle, an officer offered honourable surrender. The response was a musket shot which dropped him dead upon the deck, followed by a flow of taunts from the handful of survivors aboard the *San Mateo* about the English refusal to grapple.

It was soon after this that the *San Martin* led a group of ships to the rescue of the two isolated galleons, at which the English turned their attention to this force for a while, inflicting further damage on the flagship, before eventually breaking off the action.

In the ensuing period of respite, boats were sent to both the Portuguese vessels to take off those crew members still alive, but Diego Pimentel and a number of others declined to leave the *San Mateo*, Pimental requesting that experts be sent from the flagship to see if his ship could be saved. Although the *San Martin* herself was still leaking badly, the duke despatched a pilot and a diver, loath as he was to spare the latter with several holes in his hull still to be plugged. But by the time their pinnace had been launched, the sea had risen and the wind had shifted to the north-west, so that the crippled galleon could only be distantly discerned, drifting towards the shallows of Zeeland. When she was finally taken by the Zeelanders she was found to have been shot through no fewer than 350 times. But even then the taking was no formality, because according to William Borlas, who was on the spot, the *San Mateo* fought off her would-be captors for two hours, wounding a number of them before ultimately surrendering.

The prisoners included Pimental, heir to the Marquis de Tavara, another marquis's son, and several other men of good standing. 'I was the means that the best sort were saved,' Borlas reported chillingly to Sir Francis Walsingham, 'the rest were cast overboard and slain at the entry.'

Two Englishmen were among those who died, he added, one of them a brother of Lord Montagu. Ironically, the Catholic Lord Montagu had recently paraded before Queen Elizabeth with 200 retainers to demonstrate his loyalty to the Crown.

Meanwhile the other cripple, the *San Felipe*, managed to get alongside one of the *urcas* and begin to transfer her survivors, but in the middle of this operation, someone shouted that the *urca* was sinking, at which the *San Felipe*'s commander, Francisco de Toledo, leapt back aboard his ship together with her captain. In fact she was not sinking, but in the rising sea the waterlogged galleon was quickly carried away towards the coast, ultimately running ashore between Nieuport and Ostend.

In memory of the Gravelines battle, the banner from one of these wrecked ships was set up in the main church in the Dutch town of Leyden, it reached from the roof to the floor.

The loss to the Armada of those two great ships is the most precisely detailed event to emerge from the confusion of that day's fighting, although in the worsening weather, a Biscayan went down in full view of the *Hope*. She was the *Maria Juan*, a medium-sized ship of twenty-four guns, and earlier she had been in collision with another Spaniard, after which she was attacked by the *Hope*. Only 80 of her crew of 270 were rescued when she foundered.

Apart from the vessels wrecked on the coasts of Ireland and Scotland, no one can be sure how many Armada ships disappeared on the long voyage home, but it seems probable that some of these also foundered, simply because they were too fragile for northern seas. The English vessels, and numerous of the Spaniards, were clinker built, i.e. with each plank in the hull overlapping its neighbour, but a number of Armada vessels, the Levant squadron in particular, were carvel built for calmer

Mediterranean waters. This method of construction entailed laying the boards flush against one another, as with floorboards, but in heavy seas the seams of such vessels were liable to come apart, with dire results.

But for all the fury of the Gravelines battle, only three Spanish galleons seem to have been lost, bringing the Armada's total losses to just six vessels. Six from a force of more than sixty fighting ships – the English were, indeed, plucking their feathers 'by little and little'.

It was not from want of effort or daring that more had not been sunk, time and again Lord Howard's ships had cut off individual Spaniards and raked them through and through, sometimes closing to within a pike's length, according to one contemporary historian. But those Tudor cannons were crude weapons, and the English gunners were learning their trade in each new battle, so although a dozen or more Armada ships may have ended the day with shattered rigging and leaking hulls, they survived to sail, if not to fight, another day.

It had been an incredible battle, though; at one moment there was the sight of a Levanter with blood pouring from her scuppers as she heeled away, her gunners dead about their ordnance, but her musketeers still at their posts. In another incident, a gentleman-adventurer aboard Sir Francis Drake's ship had his bed shot from beneath him as he rested after a particularly sharp encounter; while, on board another Englishman, a cannon ball smashed into the cabin where the Earl of Northumberland and a friend were at dinner, grazed their feet, and knocked down two others standing nearby.

By late afternoon, just before a sudden storm blew up, the English might have contemplated a considerable victory as the Armada was driven into increasing disarray, but the squall which blanketed both fleets for some fifteen minutes gave the Spaniards time to recover their formation.

None the less, they lost 600 dead that day, and had 800 wounded, on their own admission. Numerous others were taken prisoner.

On the English side, casualties were minimal. 'God hath mightily protected her Majesty's forces with the least losses that ever hath been heard of within the compass of so great volleys of shot,' declared Captain George Fenner. 'I verily believe there is not three-score men lost.'

In addition to their shortage of long-range guns, another reason why the Spaniards inflicted so little damage was probably due to the poor quality of their ammunition. Research has shown that inferior production methods resulted in brittle shot which disintegrated on impact, thus severely reducing its penetrative force.

Without doubt, then, the English had the better of that day, and although in terms of numbers, the Armada was still a great force, it was, in fact, a spent force, with almost all its powder and shot exhausted, and victuals running low. If any aboard were inclined to congratulation on having survived through that tumultuous day, they were not to know that the worst, by far, was yet to be.

15   *'The Most Fearful Day in the World'*

After the battle of Gravelines the two navies never exchanged another shot – they had virtually none left, anyway – and yet the next day, Tuesday, 9 August, the Armada found itself in greater peril than at any time since departing from Lisbon. If disaster had been avoided by a hair's-breadth a few days earlier on those sinister Owers shoals off the Isle of Wight, then the Spaniards' next escape must have been by a barely measurable margin.

Exhausted as they were after the day-long Gravelines fight, hardly a man slept during the stormy night which followed – the wind had gone round to the north-west and was blowing strongly, which meant that the entire Armada was being driven towards the extensive area of shoals north of Dunkirk known as the Zeeland banks.

'... We went all along wondering when we should strike one of those banks,' declared Padre Geronimo, one of the tribe of religious men with the fleet.

With English ships to windward and the Zeeland banks to leeward, the Spaniard's plight was, indeed, acute.

'It was the most fearful day in the world,' declared Don Luis de Miranda, 'for all the people were now in utter despair of a happy issue, and stood waiting for death.'

As close to the wind as those heavy Armada ships might sail, nothing availed, relentlessly they found themselves driven shorewards.

'What shall we do, we are lost,' the Duke of Medina Sidonia is reported to have shouted to the commander of the Guipuzcoan squadron, Miguel de Oquendo, as his vessel came alongside.

'Ask Diego Flores,' came the sarcastic reply. 'As for me, I am going to fight and die like a man. Send me a supply of shot.'

Soon after dawn it had looked as if the duke would be faced with yet another battle as the English began to make towards the *San Martin* and the half dozen other vessels, those of Recalde and de Leyva among them, which stood well to windward of the rest of the Armada.

This group had gone about to face the English but they were really in no condition to do anything significant, as Medina Sidonia was all too painfully aware. 'Nearly all our trustworthy ships were unfit to resist an attack,' he reported, 'both because of the damage the gunfire had done, and because of their lack of shot.'

Fortunately for the Spaniards, Lord Howard's ships were little better off, and so after making a feint towards the duke's force, they turned away.

To some among the Armada, that failure to attack was more alarming than an attack itself, because it suggested that the English knew the Spanish ships were doomed to destruction and merely intended to be witnesses.

All morning the wind drove the Spaniards shorewards, so that by early afternoon the lead showed a mere seven fathoms of water, little more than forty feet. And since many of the galleons drew thirty feet of water, the fleet was literally minutes from disaster.

'The duke was advised that if he wanted to escape with his life he would have to surrender, it was impossible to avoid being driven aground,' reported Captain Alonzo Vanegas, who was on the poop deck of the *San Martin* at the time. He replied that he trusted in God and His Blessed Mother to bring him to a port of safety; he would not question the faith of his ancestors. People appealed to his conscience not to allow so many souls to be lost by shipwreck, but he would not listen to such advice and told them to speak no more of the matter.'

According to Vanegas, Medina Sidonia then summoned the pilots, an Englishman and a Fleming among them, but to judge from the duke's own relation of events, they can have brought him scant comfort. They told him, bleakly, 'that it was not possible to save a single ship of the Armada, for that with the wind as it was, they must all needs go on the banks of Zeeland; that God alone could prevent it.'

There was now just six-and-a-half fathoms beneath the flagship, less under some of the more leeward ships; the entire fleet seemed doomed indeed. The duke took confession with his officers and prepared to die.

Then the miracle happened, the wind quite suddenly veered to the south-west, Medina Sidonia's belief in the faith of his ancestors was triumphantly vindicated, and the fleet stood away to the north with not a single vessel driven aground.

There was, however, to be at least one Spanish casualty that day, as was witnessed by the crew of the *Hope* and reported by Lord Howard. The *Hope* came upon the unnamed Armada galleon in dire straits, and her captain, Robert Crosse, was in the process of negotiating conditions of surrender when the Spaniard simply went down. There is no record of casualties.

It was at the end of this day, as the English followed the Spaniards into the North Sea, that the brief and heady period of action enjoyed by Lord Henry Seymour's squadron was brought to an end. Much to his disgust, Seymour was ordered to resume his humdrum station in the Narrow Seas lest, in spite of all that had happened, the Duke of Parma should decide to make a dash for England.

According to the squadron's second-in-command, Sir William Wynter, they were told to drop away at dusk so that the Armada would not notice this significant reduction in the English fleet. (In fact, their departure was noted well enough despite these precautions, the Spaniards still thinking it was Hawkins' squadron.) And loath as Seymour may have been to quit, there seem to have been plenty of other captains only too anxious to go home, if Wynter is to be believed.

'Truly,' he reported to Sir Francis Walsingham, 'we had much ado with the staying of many ships that would have returned with us.'

These were almost certainly auxiliaries, and Wynter, like most regular officers of the navy, had a pretty poor opinion of auxiliaries. 'If you had seen that which I have seen of the simple service that hath been done by the merchant and coast ships,' he wrote to Walsingham, 'you would have said that we had been little holpen by them, otherwise than they did make a show.'

Undoubtedly those royal vessels fashioned by John Hawkins had played the major role, but the sheer number of ships which eventually made up the English force must have had a psychological impact on the Spaniards, whether or not the bulk of them did much fighting.

By the standards of the 1580s, the battles themselves had been fierce, that was unquestionable. 'Some Spaniards that we have taken, that were in the fight at Lepanto,' reported Lord Howard, 'do say that the worst of our four fights did exceed far the fight they had there; and they say that at some of our fights they had 20 times as much great shot there plied as they had there.'

The Lord Admiral's report to Walsingham indicated that in the fight off Gravelines, the English in fact sank three ships and so damaged four others that 'they were not able to live at sea', and so were driven ashore.

All in all, as the Armada was driven helplessly northwards, a mood of relieved self-congratulation spread throughout the English fleet, and Lord Howard was plainly one to indulge himself in that mood. The renegade Cardinal Allen had frequently asserted that the conquest of England would be a simple matter because most of the queen's ships were in a state of decay, and this had been seized on by proponents of King Philip's enterprise, now the Lord Admiral was intent on driving home the fallacy of such a belief. He urged upon Walsingham that when next writing to the English ambassador in Paris, 'I pray write to him that he will let Mendoza (the Spanish ambassador) know that her Majesty's rotten ships dare meet with his master's sound ships, and in buffeting them, though they were three great ships to one of us, yet we have shortened them 16 or 17, whereof there is three of them a-fishing in the bottom of the seas.'

Precisely how these figures were arrived at is not to be known, and one has to bear in mind that instant claims of enemy losses are frequently shown by later evidence to have been over-optimistic, as was demonstrated at the time of the Battle of Britain, when far fewer German planes were actually shot down than was claimed. On the other hand, Lord Howard was there at the centre of things, and no one else among the English would have been any better placed to know the true situation.

Francis Drake was just as euphoric as the commander-in-chief; 'There never was anything better than seeing the enemy flying with a southerly wind to the northwards,' he told Walsingham. 'I doubt not – so to handle the matter with the Duke of Sidonia as he shall wish himself at St Mary Port among his orange trees.'

There were, however, frustrations to be set alongside the triumphs, victuals were yet again extremely low, and there was, of course, practically no shot left, despite Drake's confident assertions as to what he would do to Medina Sidonia. But even more frustrating and irritating than these shortages must have been the memorandum received by Lord Howard from the Privy Council at this time.

It was the sort of document which has probably been issued to fighting men from desk-bound bureaucrats since war began, but that fact can have been of small consolation to the Lord Admiral.

The Council demanded a mass of detailed administrative information about numbers of ships, crews, victuals, ammunition, the amount of powder and shot used in one day (as if this were a constant figure), Spanish losses, English losses, location of prisoners, amounts of treasure seized – on and on the list went. But if Howard was annoyed by what was required of him up to that point, he must have been infuriated by the final question.

'What causes are there why the Spanish navy hath not been boarded by the Queen's ships?' the memorandum asked. 'And though some of the ships of Spain may be thought too huge to be boarded by the English, yet some of the Queen's ships are thought very able to have boarded divers of the meaner ships of the Spanish navy.'

The Lord Admiral seems never to have wasted time with a reply, so the arm-chair strategists at court would have been treated with the disdain they merited. None the less, that final question earned the contempt of everyone who had the slightest idea of reality, not least Sir Walter Raleigh.

Lord Howard, he asserted in his 'History of the World', was 'better advised than many malignant fools were that found fault with his demeanour. The Spaniards had an army aboard them, and he had none; they had more ships than he had and of higher building and charging, so that had he entangled himself with those great and powerful vessels, he had greatly endangered this kingdom of England ... But our admiral knew his advantage, and held it.'

However precarious the Armada's situation might have been at this time, at least its commander was not required to deal with that sort of irritating memoranda from on high, since he was now cut off from all external communication.

On the evening of the 9th, as the wind which earlier in the day had carried the Spanish fleet away from the Zeeland banks continued to freshen, the duke had called a meeting of his war council to discuss the next move, making it clear that just about every one of the fighting ships was crying out for fresh supplies of shot.

The question to be decided was whether the fleet should return to the Channel despite the continued uncertainty about Parma's readiness, or return to Spain by way of the North Sea. Whatever Medina Sidonia himself may have felt, given the composition of the council it was inevitable that the decision would be taken to return to the Channel – weather permitting.

But if the weather did not permit, if the wind, now getting up towards a gale, persisted from the south-west, then, it was agreed, there would be nothing for it but to run for home by way of Scotland 'seeing there was such great lack of provisions,' according to the duke, 'and that the ships were spoiled and unable, that hitherto had resisted the enemy.'

Spoiled and unable many of them indeed were; the *San Martin*, for example, was plugged with lead and tow to stop a gaping hold from a 50 lb shot just above the water line, but she still leaked. Juan de Recalde's ship was in little better condition, riddled with shot and with a mainmast too weakened to bear sail, while the *San Marcos*, another great galleon from the duke's squadron of Portuguese ships, had to be strapped together with cables passed under her keel.

Some of the carvel-built Levanters were in even worse plight, and three of them were simply to disappear in the next few days.

But despite the Armada's dire condition, the rumours beginning to fly around Europe all said the same thing – the Spaniards had given the English a thorough beating, victory was theirs. Even King Philip was inclined to believe it for a while.

16   *The Rumour War*

On the strength of the Armada's supposed triumphs, the Spanish ambassador to the Vatican, Count de Olivares, decided on yet another approach to Pope Sixtus concerning that gift of one million gold ducats. And to bolster his case, he was accompanied on this occasion by a friendly cardinal, one Carrafa by name.

'Carrafa addressed him in terms that would have moved any other heart,' the ambassador subsequently reported to the King of Spain, 'but the Pope only shrugged his shoulders, for when it comes to getting money out of him, it is like squeezing his life-blood ...'

Sixtus's scepticism was firmly enough grounded, but any man of a less flinty nature might well have been carried along by those confident assertions of Spanish successes and at least agreed to dole out something on account. Conceivably, of course, the Pope was all too aware from what source the assertions sprang, and had his own opinions concerning their reliability. For the fount of all this euphoria was none other than King Philip's ambassador to Paris, Don Bernardino de Mendoza, and Don Bernardino seems to have been nothing if not an optimist.

It took more than a week for mail to travel from Paris to Madrid, so that from about the middle of August, the Spanish king became the recipient of a series of reports on the Armada, all of them telling of famous victories, and all of them supplied by Mendoza.

The first was written on 9 August, the day when the entire Spanish fleet was being swept towards the Zeeland banks, and it told of a magnificent victory on 2 August, the day of the Portland battle. The news had come from one of Mendoza's agents based in Rouen, and was founded on reports from both Dieppe and Le Havre, where other Spanish spies had talked to fishermen returning from the Newfoundland grounds. How much Spanish gold was expended to obtain the information is not to be known, but certainly the Frenchmen gave good value for whatever they received.

They had, they said, been there on the spot when the battle raged – twenty-four hours it lasted – and they could report that no fewer than fifteen English ships had been sunk, including the flagship, while a number of others had been captured and scuttled.

And that was not all, because according to one witness, the mighty Drake himself had been bested. This man claimed that his barque had been close to Drake's ship when it had been sunk by one of the galleasses, and he had positively seen the Englishman flee in a small boat.

With such thrilling evidence to hand, Mendoza despatched an exultant letter to his master, a letter which gave not the slightest credence to doubt.

The response from King Philip was, predictably, more restrained, 'As you consider the news to be true,' he wrote, 'I am hopeful that it will prove to be so ... I am looking anxiously for the confirmation.'

There was more encouraging information for Mendoza a couple of days later, when his Rouen correspondent reported that the battle of Gravelines had brought further success, with many English ships sunk, others captured, and fifteen more disabled.

It was all vastly encouraging, so much so that Mendoza could not restrain himself from charging into church, rapier in hand, with cries of 'Victory, victory'.

He also had a bonfire built in the courtyard of his embassy, ready to be fired once the Spanish triumphs were confirmed.

When the true state of things ultimately emerged, Mendoza found himself the butt of half of Paris, with people sarcastically requesting him to favour them with grants of land and property in England, in view of Spain's great successes.

Before that happened, however, there was to be a welter of other reports concerning Spanish successes, including one from the French ambassador in London, who reported seven English ships sunk in the Isle of Wight battle, among them the three biggest in the queen's navy, and another from the indefatigable Rouen contact which again spoke of significant English losses, together with the fact that Sir Francis Drake's legs had been shattered by a cannon ball.

Mendoza finally lit his bonfire on the news that Drake had been captured while attempting to board Medina Sidonia's flagship.

To counter this torrent of rumours, the English ambassador in Paris, Sir Edward Stafford, had 400 pamphlets printed, giving the English version of events, but such was the pro-Spanish tide at that moment that he had difficulty in getting them distributed, as Mendoza was pleased to tell King Philip.

'The English ambassador here had some fancy news printed stating that the English had been victorious, but the people would not allow it to be sold, as they say it is all lies,' he told the king. 'One of the ambassador's secretaries began to read in the palace a relation which he said had been sent from England, but the people were so enraged that he was obliged to fly for his life.'

The position of Sir Edward Stafford himself may well have been highly ambiguous at this time because it has long been suspected that he was, in fact, a Spanish spy, the 'Julio' frequently referred to in Mendoza's letters to King Philip during the months preceding the Armada's arrival. He is suspected of regularly handing over despatches from London in exchange for money, although positive proof has never been established.

Certainly the Spanish ambassador ran a sophisticated espionage operation from his Paris embassy, its tentacles extending all across Europe. He had been expelled as the envoy to London in 1583 for his involvement with Catholic conspirators, but much of his spy network in England seems to have remained intact, so that he was able to keep King Philip reliably informed about developments in the country all the time the Armada crisis was mounting.

As the summer of 1588 merged into autumn, and the Spanish fleet had long departed from the Channel, Mendoza's correspondents appeared to be telling him only the news he wanted to hear. They said, for example, that no fewer than forty English ships had been lost in an encounter off Newcastle; they said that the Spaniards were safely anchored in a Scottish port, or 'at a very fertile Norwegian island where they will find an abundance of victuals without resistance.'

Even in late September, King Philip was still receiving optimistic reports. As the surviving Armada ships were straggling in to home ports, their crews more dead than alive, Mendoza assured his master that the fleet was, in fact, heading back towards the Channel, ready for new combat and with many prizes including twelve warships.

'Nothing of this is true,' the king scrawled wearily on the margin of this despatch, 'It will be well to tell him so.'

Another in anxious communication with King Philip was the Duke of Parma. After the Armada's abrupt departure from Calais, no one at Parma's Bruges headquarters seems to have had any idea what had happened to it until the king's illegitimate son, the Prince of Ascoli, arrived to report the Gravelines battle.

The prince was serving aboard the *San Martin* and should therefore have been in the battle himself, but on the night of the fireships' raid he had been sent round the Armada in a pinnace to warn captains to be on the alert, and after the confusion of the raid, never succeeded in catching up with the fleet again. He had, however, got close enough to observe the following day's fighting before going ashore at Dunkirk.

He was never able to rejoin the fleet, although on the word of an Italian member of the Armada captured in Ireland, he was long believed to have been drowned there.

As to the Duke of Parma, with the wind from the south he must have realized that the Spanish fleet was unlikely to get back to the coast of Flanders, and that, in consequence, he had some awkward explaining to do to King Philip.

According to a member of his staff, when the duke first received news of the Armada's approach from Spain he behaved as if he did not believe it could be true, and in some ways his subsequent actions suggest he never managed to reconcile himself to the reality of events.

He was not alone in his surprise, however, because by late July, many so-called experts in England were also confident the Armada would not come, not in 1588, anyhow, it was too late in the season for an invasion. Hence the uncomfortable surprise of some when it did materialize.

The anger of the Armada at Parma's unreadiness would have been all too clear to him from the reaction of the Inspector

General, Jorge Manrique, who had been sent ashore by the
Duke of Medina Sidonia soon after the arrival at Calais. He had
been bitterly critical of the state of affairs discovered at
Dunkirk, no supplies aboard the landing craft, no ammunition,
nothing, and when he reached headquarters at Bruges, he
took no pains to conceal his disgust. The result was that
confrontation in which the infuriated Parma was only prevented
by some of his staff from striking Manrique.

What must have particularly concerned the general about this
incident was that when he ordered the Inspector General to
return to the Armada, he was curtly told by Manrique that he
would not do so until he had reported the situation to King
Philip.

Thus the duke found it immediately expedient to sit down and
dictate for the king's perusal, a not altogether convincing
justification of his behaviour.

His first letter was dated 8 August, the day of the Gravelines
battle, and the day after the row with Manrique. 'The men who
have recently come hither from the Duke,' he reported, 'not
seeing the boats armed or with any artillery on board, and men
not shipped, have been trying to make out we are not ready.
They are in error.'

The boats had been ready for months, Parma insisted, and
even though there were not as many seamen available as there
ought to be, men could be embarked in very short time. What
they could not do, he repeated, was go out and join in the
fighting, as the Duke of Medina Sidonia was still expecting them
to do.

On the day that letter was written, Parma took himself to
Dunkirk, where the long deserted embarkation areas were
suddenly alive with troops as he sought to demonstrate the
extent of his preparedness. It was a totally useless exercise, of
course, a mere charade aimed at self-justification, because not
only was the Armada itself nowhere to be seen, but weather
conditions were all wrong and many of the barges were simply
not ready for their task.

'The day on which we were to embark we found the vessels
still unfinished, not a pound of cannon aboard, and nothing to
eat,' Don Juan Manrique told the king's secretary in a letter
dated 11 August. But Don Juan clearly took a far more
sympathetic view of the matter than did his namesake Don Jorge

Manrique. 'This was not because the Duke of Parma failed to use every possible effort,' he went on, 'but because both the seamen and those who had to carry out the details, openly and undisguisedly directed their energies not to serve his Majesty.'

As with most armies of occupation, the Spanish force in Flanders had obviously encountered a good deal of passive resistance from the local inhabitants, as the troops quickly realized when they stepped aboard the unarmed, leaking hulks in which they were expected to cross to England. But if Parma was not play-acting when he put his men aboard, then he was guilty of serious negligence in not ascertaining the true condition of his fleet.

The simple fact seems to have been that from the beginning of 1588, once his force was almost halved by sickness, the duke's enthusiasm for King Philip's great enterprise waned rapidly. Had the Armada been able to sweep the Narrow Seas totally clear of English ships, had Count Justin of Nassau not had a flotilla of flyboats ready to pounce at the first appearance of Parma's fleet, and had winds, tides and weather all combined to provide perfect conditions, then those 17,000 remaining troops of the duke's army might, just might, have set foot on English soil.

But since not one of those conditions was fulfilled in that early-August period, and since the unremitting southerly winds after the Gravelines battle would clearly not permit the Spanish fleet to return, Parma had soon gone back to Bruges, leaving orders for his shoal of landing craft to be dismantled.

'No one can be more grieved than I am,' he told King Philip in reviewing the entire fiasco, 'I will only say therefore that this must come from the hand of the Lord, who knows well what He does, and can redress it all, rewarding your Majesty with many victories and the full fruition of your desires, in His own good time.'

Since every aspect of the Armada venture was attributed to the will of God, it would have been difficult for the king to challenge Parma's sentiments, convenient as they may have been to excuse his actions.

Even so, the duke was still finding it necessary to justify his conduct as 1588 drew to a close. Writing to the king's secretary he stressed yet again that his men had been ready – 16,000 already embarked at Nieuport, he claimed (a suspiciously large

number) and others ready to embark at Dunkirk on 7 August,
the day the Armada lay off Calais.

Everything could have gone ahead, he insisted, but for the
flight of the Spanish fleet.

17   *Tilbury – 'This Place Breedeth Courage'*

Although the last Armada battle had taken place on 8 August,
and the Spaniards had commenced their inadvertent northerly
flight the following day, it was not until the 18th that the queen
and her ministers heard a word about what had happened.

The story was carried to Elizabeth by the Earl of Cumberland,
he who had dashed away with Robert Cary in search of a ship
some two weeks earlier when the first news of the Armada
reached London. And had his arrival before the queen been
stage-managed it could hardly have been better done, because
when Cumberland bent his knee to the monarch and handed her
the despatch he bore from Lord Howard, she had just made her
historic rallying cry to some 20,000 of her troops assembled at
Tilbury.

Cumberland, in fact, brought good and bad tidings to the
Tilbury camp, the good being the flight of the Armada, the bad,
a report that not only had the Duke of Parma at last got his
army together, but that his troops were already embarked and
on their way to England.

This latter story, springing from Parma's belated activity at
Dunkirk and Nieuport, was believed for a few days, and like
most unscotched rumours, grew in stature with the passage of
the hours.

Two days after it had been told to the queen, the compiler of a
professional newsletter confidently informed a client, 'Our news

on Friday was certain – that the Prince was embarked with 50,000 foot and 6,000 horse.' He was imminently expected in England on the prevailing spring tides, the writer went on to aver.

Hearing that Parma had stirred himself, Queen Elizabeth initially felt honour-bound to remain with her troops in case the Spaniards did, indeed, invade – 'Thus,' declared Walsingham, reporting from Tilbury to Lord Burghley, 'your Lordship seeth that this place breedeth courage' – but, possibly considering she would be more hindrance than help, her generals seem to have persuaded her to a change of mind, and she left for London that evening.

Her two-day visit to the army had, though, been a splendid personal triumph as well as what, in today's terms, would be described as a highly competent public relations exercise. Among the 20,000 men encamped at Tilbury it is fair to assume that only a handful would ever have set eyes on the queen before, and not many more would have even known what she looked like.

She was fifty-six at the time, old in an age of rampant mortality, her smallpox-ravaged face generally thick with powder to disguise the marks of that illness and the lines of age. Yet such was the lustre attaching to her person that ancient, black-toothed, red-wigged as she was, she aroused in her soldiers such a pitch of patriotism that just about every man there would willingly have given his life in defence of queen and country.

'Her presence and princely encouragement,' reported a contemporary historian, 'infused a second spirit of love, loyalty and resolution into every soldier in her army, who being (as it were) ravished with their Sovereign's sight, all – prayed heartily the Spaniards might land quickly, and when they knew they were fled, began to lament.'

The success of Queen Elizabeth's visit must have been particularly gratifying to her old favourite the Earl of Leicester, because he had invited her in the first place, and as he had been at pains to emphasize to Walsingham, her Secretary, the organization of the Tilbury camp had fallen, *faute de mieux*, almost totally on him.

Leicester's considerable self-esteem would thus have been compensated for the affront suffered earlier by the government's failure to inform him personally of Lord Howard's first successes against the Armada, and for the infuriating fact that his two principal lieutenants, Sir John Norris and Sir Roger Williams, had both taken themselves elsewhere when they should have been at Tilbury assisting him.

'If you saw how weakly I am assisted,' he had complained to Walsingham, 'you would be sorry to think that we here should be the front against the enemy, that is so mighty, if he should land here.'

Any contemporary of Leicester's with a knowledge of soldiering was more likely to have been sorry that he was in command of the camp than that he was so weakly aided, because both Norris and Williams were much more able soldiers and could well have found themselves seriously handicapped by the earl's incompetence, had the Spaniards arrived.

He himself had formed some pretty firm ideas about the effectiveness of some classes of citizens among his troops, and had taken an early decision to get rid of all the gentlemen farmers, on the grounds that they were too used to easy living.

'Those rich men which have been daintily fed and warm lodged,' he declared, 'when they came hither to lie abroad in the fields, were worse able to endure the same than any others.'

He thus decreed that they should return to their farms – it was harvest time, anyway – and send either a son or a paid substitute.

Leicester's views on Londoners as soldiers were not much more approving. The men from the City had apparently been agitating to serve under captains they knew, which did nothing to endear them to their irascible general. 'For your Londoners,' he wrote testily to Walsingham, 'I see as the matter stands, their service will be little except they have their own captains, and having them, I look for none at all by them when we shall meet the enemy. I know what burghers be, well enough.'

As for the captains themselves, there was some disgruntlement at Tilbury because a number of them who had been recalled from the Netherlands to season the raw militia with their battle experience found that there were not enough units for everyone to get a command, and thus they lost pay and perks.

A captain's perks could be considerable, the most profitable usually being illegal. There were complaints after the Tilbury camp broke up, for example, that some had swindled their men over pay, while others were accused of charging up to £5 – roughly £400 at today's rates – to allow men to buy themselves out of service.

Deserters were always a problem in Tudor times, as were men buying themselves out or hiring substitutes. 'For my life,' declared a despairing Sir Thomas Mulsho concerning such practices among his men, 'I cannot persuade them to keep their money in their purses but they will either be hiring of men in their places or else bribing to get themselves released. I am at my wits end ...'

Not everyone went unwillingly to Tilbury, however, in fact the great majority, without the slightest concept of what war entailed, seem to have travelled to the camp with a sense of high adventure, if the historian, John Stow, is to be believed. He actually witnessed troops on their way to Tilbury, noting 'their cheerful countenances, courageous words and gestures, dancing and leaping.'

The men had been assigned to the camp with a view to confronting any Spanish landing in the Thames estuary, but since Parma's instructions were to approach London from south of the river, they were encamped on the wrong side to have quickly impeded him. The assembly of so many men in a matter of days soon led to shortages of supplies and, initially, to profiteering, and so a royal proclamation had to be issued which laid down a list of prices for food and accommodation within a twenty-mile radius of Tilbury. It also required a minimum supper menu to be drawn up by lodging-house keepers, and for a maxium charge of threepence a meal – about £1 today.

For those troops who found lodgings in the area, one penny a night, or sixpence a week, got them a feather bed, while a double feather bed cost twopence a week more. A flock bed could be had for fourpence a week.

The chronic shortage of state funds which had kept the navy low on victuals and shot also had its effect on the land forces, so that at no time during the Armada crisis was the militia mustered in the numbers which the nation's defence plans called for.

'I beseech you assemble your forces and play not away this kingdom by delays,' Leicester urgently appealed to the queen's Secretary, but his words made little impact, and the force of

15,000 men which should have formed a reserve army within easy reach of London was never brought up to strength.

Luckily for Elizabeth and her ministers, their tardiness proved justified, and had the added advantage of saving a good deal of money in terms of the militia's pay. All the same, it was a gamble, and had a Spanish force actually invaded, there must have been some disastrous gaps in England's defences.

The queen's personal safety was another matter of concern to many Englishmen, and the gentlemen of Dorset are said to have offered the tempting sum of £500 (£40,000 today) for the privilege of undertaking that task. Given her never-ending need of money, it must have been difficult for Elizabeth to turn down such an offer, but turn it down she appears to have done because the bodyguard of 1,200 foot and 100 cavalry which her cousin, Lord Hunsdon, got together seems not to have included the Dorset men.

Only a handful of Lord Hunsdon's force would have travelled with the queen to Tilbury, however, because the visit was made by river. Nevertheless, accompanied as she was by her full complement of yeoman of the guard, together with such gentlemen pensioners of the household who were not with Lord Howard's fleet, the retinue must have presented an impressive spectacle to the impressionable troops as it stepped ashore at Tilbury.

To add to the glamour of the occasion, the queen had ascended the steep hill on which the camp was pitched in a jewel-encrusted coach, the jewels set in a chequer pattern amid knots of wrought gold. Having gained the camp, itself bright with the multi-coloured tents of the nobles and gentry, and the green booths where the troops slept, the monarch would have surveyed a panoramic sweep of the countryside through which flowed the broad Thames, and would presumably have complimented her generals on selecting such an excellent location – albeit on the wrong bank of the river.

As her coach drove among the ranks of the militia, pikes and flags were dipped in salute and the troops fell to their knees and cried blessings upon her. So vehement was their performance, in fact, that messengers had to be sent ahead to request the remainder of the force not to be quite so noisily enthusiastic.

Enclosed as she had been in her coach that first day, many of the troops must have received little more than a fleeting impression of their great and mystical sovereign, but on the second day, that matter was dramatically rectified. From her lodging, a mile or two from Tilbury camp, Elizabeth appeared mounted on a large white horse, which she later presented to Lord Burghley – a portrait of it is still to be seen at Hatfield House. She wore on this occasion a velvet dress as white as the horse itself, and in her hand she carried a symbolic silver truncheon; a plume of feathers topped her hair. She had come to see, and to be seen, so that her escort was cut to a handful of officers, Leicester among them, preceded by ten scarlet-clad trumpeters and the Earl of Ormonde, bearing the Sword of State.

After parading herself before the entire army in a tour of inspection, she reviewed a march past of the force. And it was from the reviewing point that she delivered her historic exhortation, probably the most memorable words ever uttered by an English monarch.

Given the number of troops present, and the fact that there existed no such thing as a public address system, one wonders how many men even heard a single word she uttered, let alone made sense of what she was saying. And that, perhaps, accounts for the fact that at least three independent reports of her speech have come down through the years, each much different from the others.

The best known is so well constructed as to suggest either that it was copied from the original script the queen used, or that it was carefully worked over by a skilled hand at some later stage. As it stands it reads like a speech which even Shakespeare might have been proud to have written, rousing and defiant, perfectly suited to the occasion.

'My loving people,' it began, 'we have been persuaded by some that are careful of our safety to take heed of how we commit ourselves to armed multitudes for fear of treachery. But I assure you I do not desire to live to distrust my faithful and loving people. Let tyrants fear! I have always so behaved myself that under God I have placed my chief strength and safeguard in the loyal hearts and goodwill of my subjects. And therefore I am come amongst you, as you see, at this time, not for my recreation and disport; but being resolved in the midst of the heat of the battle to live or die amongst you all; to lay down for my God, and for my Kingdom and for my people, my honour, and my blood even, in the dust.

'I know I have the body but of a weak and feeble woman; but I have the heart and stomach of a King, and of a King of England, too, and think foul scorn that Parma or Spain or any Prince of Europe should dare to invade the borders of my realm; to which, rather than any dishonour shall grow by me, I myself will take up arms, I myself will be your general, judge and rewarder of every one of your virtues in the field. I know already for your forwardness you deserve rewards and crowns; and we do assure you, in the word of a prince, they shall be duly paid to you.'

No matter who composed that speech, the queen herself or some anonymous court official, their words produced the desired result, with those who had heard and understood them raising the first tumultuous cheers, and the cheering spreading on and on throughout the 20,000 like wind rippling across a field of grain.

Had the Spaniards appeared at that moment, the English would have fallen upon them with the fury of men intoxicated by patriotism.

Queen Elizabeth departed later that day, and perhaps when she had gone the outlook seemed less roseate, particularly when a violent thunderstorm blew up an hour or so afterwards.

The camp was maintained for about a further week, and then, with the Armada far to the north, and Parma known to be no longer an imminent threat, it was disbanded. Mid-August was, after all, the peak of the harvest season.

There is an echo of Tilbury to be discovered in Great St Helen's church, Bishopsgate, the finest medieval parish church remaining in the City of London. It takes the form of a wall monument to the commander of the city's trained bands, one Martin Bond, 'Captain in ye yeare 1588 at ye camp at Tilbury'.

18   'In Such High Latitudes'

About the time on 18 August that the Earl of Cumberland was galloping post-haste to Tilbury to report the Armada's retreat, the crew of a fishing boat some 500 miles to the north were witnessing a truly incredible sight. The fishermen, from Southampton, had been working the rich but empty wastes of water south-east of the Shetlands, where even the appearance of another fisherman was an event, when their astonished eyes fell upon an amazing spectacle – a vast fleet, a hundred sail or more of 'monstrous great ships', just to the west of them.

It was ten days after the battle of Gravelines, and the Armada was on the last stage of its northwards course. Despite a following wind almost all the way, it was averaging little more than two knots.

The English fleet had trailed it for three days after its escape from the Zeeland banks, occasionally making as if to attack (putting on a 'brag countenance' was the way Lord Howard described it) but since victuals and shot were both almost exhausted, there was really nothing effective the Lord Admiral's ships could do. Thus with the wind continuing southerly, and the Armada clearly having nothing but survival immediately in mind, the English had been content to turn for home ports, leaving just a couple of small, swift vessels to keep watch on the Spaniards.

Around the time Lord Howard's ships began to beat south, a melancholy drama was taking place in the Armada. Because of a growing water shortage, all the horses and mules were thrown overboard. Hours later, a cargo vessel crossed the track of the Spanish fleet and reported the sea full of animals, all still swimming.

Why they were not slaughtered to boost dwindling food supplies is a puzzle, but certainly those poor, afflicted creatures could hardly have experienced a more dismal close to their lives

Spaniards instructed to sail west,
well into Atlantic, before setting
southerly course for Spain

But many make for
Ireland where 26 ships
and 5000 men are lost

SHETLANDS

ORKNEYS

HEBRIDES

SCOTLAND

DONEGAL
BAY

IRELAND

GALWAY
BAY

0   50   100 mls

The End of
the Armada

than the three weeks since the Spanish fleet left Corunna. First, the numerous alarming storms, then the truly terrifying tumult of the battles, and finally, death by drowning, after hours of hopeless swimming. If several thousand Armada crewmen were soon to experience equally miserable deaths, they at least would have known what was happening to them, and why.

To most members of the fleet, however, an incident far more dramatic than the mere jettisoning of horses had been enacted two days earlier, when a pinnace made its deliberate way among the entire assemblage of ships, a body hanging from its yard-arm. The body was that of Don Cristobal de Avila, captain of the *Santa Barbara*, one of the *urcas*, and a near neighbour of the Duke of Medina Sidonia.

He died because he had disobeyed orders, and because he did not have enough influential friends in the Armada.

Captain Francisco de Cuellar (an ancestor of the present Secretary General of the United Nations, Perez de Cuellar) had influential friends and a spirited tongue, too, otherwise he would have shared the fate of Don Cristobal.

The offence for which, on 10 August, each was instantly court-martialled and sentenced to hang was to have allowed their ships to get far ahead of the rest of the Armada, an action against which all captains had been expressly warned on two separate occasions.

Captain de Cuellar, who was soon to survive the most harrowing experiences when shipwrecked in Ireland, had, in fact, a very good answer to the charge, but had he not had infuence as well, it would probably have proved of little avail.

His Castilian ship, the *San Pedro*, had been in the thick of things throughout the Channel battles, and for ten days he had had virtually no sleep. On the day following the near disaster on the Zeeland banks, with the English offering no real threat, he had decided to sleep, only to discover on being awakened that his sailing master had taken the *San Pedro* well ahead of the rest of the fleet in order to make repairs, and that himself was consequently under arrest.

At his court martial, de Cuellar recited this story with vigour and indignation, adducing his conduct during the fighting, and vowing that if any member of his crew could point to a single thing he had done wrong, they could cut him to pieces.

The captain's performance so impressed the Judge Advocate

that he wrote at once to the duke, declining to see the sentence of hanging carried out unless he received an order bearing Medina Sidonia's own signature. The result was a command of annulment.

Although it might have been natural and entirely understandable for the Armada's commander to have made an example of one or two disobedient officers in view of the need for iron discipline on the long voyage home, it was not he but the senior army commander on the enterprise, General Francisco de Bobadilla, who pronounced the death verdicts on de Avila and de Cuellar.

The duke himself, totally exhausted following day after nerve-racking day at the taffrail of the *San Martin*, had finally taken to his sick-bed, where he was to remain for much of the long voyage home. Thus his judicial role in the death of his Andalusian neighbour seems to have been marginal, and it may be that had he been healthy, and in command, the hapless Don Cristobal would also have been reprieved.

On the other hand, a document left by the Armada's chief purser, one Pedro Coco Calderon, suggests that Medina Sidonia not only ordered this execution, but also condemned several other captains to the galleys, and reduced the rank of certain army officers, all for allowing their ships to drift away from battle stations during the fighting.

It was hardly an auspicious start to the daunting voyage which every man in the fleet knew he was facing.

For most of the first five days of the Armada's northward flight the weather was so bad, with rain-squalls, fog and heavy seas, that it was impossible to distinguish one vessel from another. When the weather briefly cleared, Purser Calderon's ship, the *San Salvador*, vice-flagship of the *urca* squadron, found itself near some fifteen other vessels, including the flagship, and Calderon obligingly supplied Medina Sidonia with rice, and certain 'hospital delicacies', which originally he had been planning to sell at a good profit. This act of altruism proved burdensome to the purser's pocket because pretty soon a message came from the duke requesting him to make similar gifts all round the Armada, so that after a few days his stocks were virtually exhausted.

There can be little doubt that the 50 lb bags of rice which

Calderon doled out were eagerly received, because in addition to the hazards which lay ahead in such cruel and unknown seas, the Armada was becoming desperately short of victuals.

'Our provisions are so scanty,' Medina Sidonia informed King Philip in a letter dated 21 August, 'that in order to make them and the water last a month, the rations of every person in this fleet, without exception, have been reduced; just enough being served to keep them alive, namely, half a pound of biscuit, a pint of water and half a pint of wine daily, without anything else. Your Majesty may imagine what suffering this entails in the midst of the discomforts of so long a voyage.'

By the time that letter was dictated there were already 3,000 sick in the Armada, in addition to the many wounded, and the sick-list was growing daily. Foul water aboard many ships was one reason for so much illness, another was lack of adequate clothing for those cold northern climes.

Round about 14 August, three Levanters are reported to have fallen away eastwards, never to be seen again, and a week or so later, another ship from the Levant squadron, the *Trinidad Valencera*, found herself one of an isolated quartet of vessels battling against headwinds somewhere north of Scotland. The other three ships in this group were all *urcas*, more accustomed to the coastal waters of the Baltic and northern Europe than these cruel Atlantic seas, and one by one they were lost.

The first to go was the *Barca de Amburg*, but there was sufficient warning to get all of her crew of 350 aboard the *Trinidad* and the flagship of the *urcas*, the *Gran Grifon*. Two nights later, on 3 September, the three remaining ships lost touch with one another in a storm, and the second surviving *urca*, the *Castillo Negro*, with a crew of nearly 300, disappeared for all time.

The *Trinidad Valencera* ran aground in Donegal some two weeks later, which left only the *Gran Grifon* still at sea. By that time, however, she too was in such a bad way that her destruction was only a matter of when and where. Her seams had opened up alarmingly after a storm on 7 September, but for almost three weeks she remained afloat, only able to sail with the wind behind her, and thus entirely at the mercy of the weather.

She was not a lucky ship, the *Gran Grifon*, because she had already suffered heavy casualties among her 300 men the morning after the Portland battle, when caught by the English well astern of the rest of the Armada. Now, hampered by the damage sustained in that attack and the springing of her seams, she was simply blown hither and thither, north, south, then north again, her crew increasingly exhausted by the constant patching and pumping.

Someone aboard the *Gran Grifon*, some anonymous diarist, kept a record of those gruesome weeks, and of the way the ordeal ended. It was the night of 26 September, and nobody knew where they were after the interminable buffeting to and fro, all they were aware of was that there seemed to be rocky shores on all sides, the breakers visible despite the darkness.

'Truly our one thought was that our lives were ended,' the unknown chronicler recorded, 'and each of us reconciled himself to God as well as he could, and prepared for the long journey of death. To have forced the ship any more would only have ended it and our lives the sooner, so we gave up trying. The poor soldiers, too, who had worked incessantly at the pumps and buckets, lost heart and let the water rise ...'

Then, just when all hope had gone, they sighted an island ahead, and with luck for once on their side, managed to find a sheltered anchorage. They had reached Fair Isle.

With a change of tide next morning, the *Gran Grifon* was driven ashore and wrecked, but all of her crew managed to scramble ashore, to begin a year-long saga of survival which will later unfold.

It was about the time in late August when the *Trinidad Valencera* and the *urcas* found themselves alone that the Duke of Medina Sidonia felt sufficiently well to dictate his letter to King Philip, a missive which touched upon the problems of food and water almost as an afterthought, and which was designed primarily as a statement in defence of his conduct subsequent to the Channel battles.

'The Armada was so completely crippled and scattered,' he reported, 'that my first duty to your Majesty seemed to save it, even at the risk we are running in undertaking this voyage, which is so long and in such high latitudes.

'Ammunition and the best of our vessels were lacking, and experience had shown how little we could depend on the ships that remained, the Queen's fleet being so superior to ours in this sort of fighting in consequence of the strength of their artillery and the fast sailing of their ships.'

That was a significant admission by the duke, because it showed it was the English navy, rather than adverse weather, which principally thwarted the Armada. For all the protestations of the Spaniards that they would have returned to the Channel had the weather permitted, the duke seems to have been only too aware that in view of its various casualties, particularly the loss of such powerful galleons as the *San Felipe* and *San Mateo*, the fleet had no answer to the new style of warfare demonstrated by Lord Howard's ships.

Medina Sidonia's letter was written at a time when the weather had worsened once more, with days of heavy gales, strong headwinds, fog and rain. Calderon, clearly a person of influence in the Armada and a man with a knowledge of the sea, went aboard the *San Martin* on the 24th, and in conversation with the duke and his adviser, Diego Flores de Valdes, suggested that Ireland should be given a wide berth, that the fleet should sail well out into the Atlantic before making south for Spain. According to Calderon's account, Diego Flores opposed this idea, although it was supported by a French pilot to whom Medina Sidonia had offered 2,000 ducats to get them safely home.

In the event, it was the course which the duke duly decreed, although numerous ships were forced to disregard it through shortage of food and water, and paid the penalty on the Irish coast.

The weather closed in yet again after that conference, so that for over a week 'we sailed without knowing whither' Calderon reported, 'through constant storms, fogs and squalls.'

When the duke wrote to King Philip again on 3 September, ninety-five ships were to be counted, and seventeen were missing, including those of Recalde and de Leyva. The wind was in the north-west by then, favourable for once, but as he stressed to his royal master, that was just a lucky chance, because the prevailing wind in those waters was from a southerly direction.

'I pray that God in His mercy will grant us fine weather so that the Armada may soon enter port,' he wrote, 'for we are so short of provisions that if for our sins we be long delayed, all will be irretrievably lost.'

The *San Martin* got back to Spain some three weeks later, but by then, all had indeed been irretrievably lost for several thousand members of the Spanish fleet.

19   A Queen's Rewards

It was as well for the English that *they* did not have to face a long voyage home when they gave up their pursuit of the Armada, because conditions aboard many ships were little less parlous than among the Spaniards. Food was very short, many men were in rags after months at sea without a single change of clothing, and sickness was everywhere.

As to the vessels themselves, following nine or ten days of fighting, and several weeks of hard sailing, most were in urgent need of overhaul.

It took about five days for the fleet to get back to ports in south-east England, battling against adverse winds and surviving yet another storm, 'a most violent storm as was ever seen at this time of year,' in Lord Howard's own words. It was so rough, in fact, that even those free of illness could not eat.

The abysmal weather brought one consolation, however, it was driving the Armada further and further to the north.

But no one could be entirely certain it would not return, there were circumstances which *could* bring it south again, the danger was by no means entirely past; thus there grew among the navy's principal officers the nagging worry that Queen Elizabeth, with her customary zeal to save money, would prematurely reduce the nation's defences.

Lord Howard certainly believed there was a strong possibility that the Armada would return, and so one of his first acts on getting into port at Margate was to despatch an urgent plea to the queen's secretary, Sir Francis Walsingham.

'I know not what you think of it at Court,' he wrote, 'but I do think, and so doth all here, that there cannot be too great forces maintained yet for five or six weeks on the seas, for although we have put the Spanish fleet past the Frith (the Firth of Forth) and I think past the Isles, yet God knoweth whether they goeth either to the Nase of Norway, or into Denmark, or to the Isles of

Orkney to refresh themselves, and so to return; for I think they dare not return (to Spain) with this dishonour and shame to their king, and overthrow of their Pope's credit. Sir, sure bind, sure find; a kingdom is a great wager.'

Francis Drake was another who feared Elizabeth's parsimony at this still critical time. 'My poor opinion is that I dare not advise her Majesty to hazard a kingdom for the saving a little charge,' he declared to Walsingham.

There were pleas from other officers, too, for the queen to keep her purse-strings loosened, pleas with which Walsingham must have concurred, since he plainly considered that penny-pinching had already done harm.

'I am sorry the Lord Admiral was forced to leave the prosecution of the enemy through the wants he sustained,' he told the Lord Chancellor. 'Our half-doings doth breed dishonour, and leaveth the disease uncured.'

Secretary Walsingham's concern for the nation's honour might have been better directed towards those who had just thwarted the Armada, because as Lord Howard discovered on returning to port, barely a thought seemed to have been given to them.

'Sickness and mortality begins wonderfully to grow among us; and it is a most pitiful sight to see, here in Margate, how the men, having no place to receive them into here, die in the streets,' he complained to Lord Burghley.

'I am driven myself, of force, to come a-land to see them bestowed in some lodging, and the best I can get is barns and such outhouses. It would grieve any man's heart to see them that have served so valiantly to die so miserably.'

As an example of how virulent shipboard diseases could be, Howard quoted the case of the *Elizabeth Jonas*, one of the fleet's three biggest ships. She had lost 200 of her crew of 500 even before the Armada arrived.

'So I was driven to set all the rest of her men ashore, to take out her ballast, and to make fires in her of wet broom, three or four days together, and so hoped thereby to have cleansed her of infection.

'Now the infection is broken out in greater extremity than ever it did before and men die and sicken faster than ever they did. We think and judge that the infection remaineth in the pitch.'

Given the almost total ignorance at that time about hygiene, and health at sea, it was not surprising that the pitch used to seal the seams of ships should be suspected of harbouring the deadly germs.

Twelve days later the situation had deteriorated alarmingly. 'The infection is now grown very great and in many ships, and now very dangerous;' the Lord Admiral informed Queen Elizabeth, 'and those that come in fresh are soonest infected; they sicken one day and die the next. It is a thing that ever followeth such great services.'

If it were a well-established fact that long weeks at sea led to such outbreaks of disease it seems all the more scandalous that no preparations whatever had been made to deal with the emergency, and that men should be left to die like dogs in the streets.

Was this the 'crowns and rewards' which in her Tilbury speech the queen had promised?

'What does a man think of when he thinks of nothing,' Elizabeth had once demanded of a courtier.

'Madam,' came the reply, 'he thinks of a woman's promise.'

Had that courtier dared to say a queen's promise, he would aptly have reflected the situation at that moment.

By the end of August, things were even worse, with some ships unable to muster enough fit men even to weigh anchor, and the suspicion growing throughout the fleet that the principal cause of all the trouble was a consignment of sour beer.

The beer crisis was yet another problem for Lord Howard, one for which he had no ready answers; 'I know not which way to deal with the mariners to make them rest contented with sour beer,' he reported to Walsingham, 'for nothing doth displease them more.'

They were just about as displeased, however, by lack of pay, because having gone without money week after week while at sea, they now found on returning to port that there was still virtually none to be had.

Once more the Lord Admiral was forced to protest at government indifference; in a letter to the Privy Council he declared, 'I must deliver unto your Lordships the great discontentment of the men here, who well hoped, after this so good service, to have received their whole pay, and finding it come this scantly to them, it breeds a marvellous alteration amongst them.'

A few days later, Lord Howard tackled Walsingham on the

same subject, avowing his intention to pay some of the men out of his own pocket in order to see them satisfied. England had not seen the last of the Spanish threat, he declared, and he wanted to ensure he had men prepared to serve with him when the Spaniards returned.

Nearly a month after the fleet docked, the government had still not made adequate preparations to relieve hardship, sick men were being sent ashore with not a penny in their pockets and many ships had no more than a day's victuals.

'It were pitiful to have men starve after such service,' Howard wrote in yet another plea to Walsingham. 'Therefore I had rather open the Queen's Majesty's purse something to relieve them, than they should be in that extremity; for we are to look to have more of these services; and if men should not be cared for better than to let them starve and die miserably, we should very hardly get men to serve.'

Although he was by no means the best able to do so, he added, he would himself find one-third of the men's pay, if the government would find the rest, because 'before God, I had rather have never penny in the world than they should lack.'

His were the sentiments of a thoroughly caring commander, but how much weight they carried is by no means clear. As late as December he was still having to haggle with the government over the costs of the Armada operation, and by then he had obviously become so fed up with the whole process that rather than face further niggardly queries and complaints, he had decided to pay for the fleet's wine and beer out of his own pocket.

During the course of her reign, Queen Elizabeth was forced to sell today's equivalent of some £72m of Crown lands to finance England's wars, so her concern for money was understandable. But when one compares her fine sentiments at Tilbury with what actually happened when the ships came home, one is entitled to question the depth of her genuine concern for her people.

Certainly the treatment which the victorious English received compares very unfavourably with that which King Philip pro vided for the defeated and demoralized survivors of the Armada when they returned home.

England was to have been a rich honeypot for the men of the Armada. 'Pray to God,' wrote one Spaniard to a relative, 'that in England he doth give me a house of some very rich merchant, where I may place my ensign; which the owner thereof do ransom of me in thirty thousand ducats.'

That was the way it should have happened, a beneficent God showering success and fortune upon the Spanish invaders, 'that I may get wherewithal to repair to my house to live at ease.'

Unfortunately for those who actually set foot on English soil, all but a handful were to endure a long and miserable sojourn, with the taste of gall in their mouths rather than the taste of honey.

When Spanish prisoners-of-war started to appear they found that returning members of Lord Howard's fleet were whipping up such hatred of Spain that they went in fear of their lives. Numerous Englishmen, particularly those who found themselves suddenly and unwillingly responsible for these Armada relics, wished to have seen them drowned in the first place – 'We would have been very glad they had been made water spaniels when they were first taken,' in the words of George Cary, of Cockington, in Devon.

In view of the fact that virtually nothing had been prepared for the aid and succour of returning members of the English fleet, it was hardly surprising that plans to cope with Spanish prisoners were even more skeletal. In fact, the Central Government seems to have had no plans whatsoever, all the arrangements and all the costs, at least initially, falling upon hapless dignitaries in the places where they were put ashore.

London's Bridewell found itself deluged with prisoners-of-war, and pretty soon its funds were exhausted, leading one of the city's aldermen to send an urgent message to Sir Francis Walsingham. If Government help were not quickly forthcoming, he stressed, it would be necessary to levy a charge on all of London's citizens, 'which will be very unwillingly assented to by the common sort.'

It would, indeed, have been the last straw for Englishmen to have paid extra taxes to succour their would-be conquerors, having paid so much to guard against them.

But it was in south-west England, where those two crippled galleons the *San Salvador* and *Nuestra Senora del Rosario* were taken into harbour, that the main problems arose.

The *San Salvador*, blown half apart by the explosion of her powder store during the first day of combat, was initially shepherded into Portland, where about 60 of the remaining 200 barrels of powder aboard her were promptly stolen, along with a quantity of ropes and casks. She was then taken to Weymouth, and as she had originally carried the Armada's Paymaster, there were high hopes among the authorities there that treasure might be still aboard. Thus an intensive search was undertaken for a 'chest of very great weight' supposedly stored in the forepeak. But even though part of the ballast was removed, not a thing was discovered.

Most of the *San Salvador*'s crew who survived the explosion had been transferred to other Armada ships before she was abandoned, and only a handful seem still to have been aboard by the time Weymouth was reached; these included two Frenchmen, four German men and one German woman. Twelve of this group of survivors died ashore, and there was concern about the rest.

'We humbly beseech your lordships to give some speedy direction what shall be done with them,' local officials appealed to the Privy Council, 'for they that are here diseased, naked and chargeable.'

It was the fact that they were chargeable, and that money expended locally might never be reimbursed by the government, which would particularly have worried the signatories of that letter.

The *San Salvador* was a big ship, one of the biggest in the Armada, and Weymouth harbour could not accommodate her; she was being transferred to Portsmouth, with a mainly English crew manning the pumps non-stop, when a storm sank her in Studland Bay. Thirty-four men were rescued, but twenty-three were drowned, including six Frenchmen and Flemings who had been with her ever since she left Lisbon.

The prisoners from the *Rosario* were a greater problem because there were far more of them, around 400. Having suddenly to find food for such a number, and to guard them, were major headaches for the authorities at Dartmouth, where the ship was berthed. The ship herself was almost bare of provisions, the small amount of fish left aboard being rotten, and the bread full of worms.

So once more, Walsingham was appealed to.

'The people's charity unto them (coming with so wicked an intent) is very cold,' wrote George Cary, 'so that if there be not order forthwith taken by your Lordships, they must starve.'

Before Walsingham or the Council could reply, 166 veterans were returned to the *Rosario*, despite the ship's shortage of food, because of the problem of guarding them when everyone was busy with the harvest.

Nearly two months later the government had still done nothing concrete about the situation, and many of the prisoners were on the edge of starvation. Cary himself had already spent £15 for their relief (about £1,200 today) and others had chipped in too, 'for otherwise they must needs have perished through hunger, and possibly thereby have bred some infection which might be dangerous to our country.'

Eventually the survivors of this incarceration were ransomed for about one month's pay each, with the exception of a handful 'of the better sort', who were exchanged for Englishmen imprisoned in Spanish jails, or serving as galley slaves.

The *Rosario* was eventually broken up, and some of her timbers are reputed to form the roof beams of Dartmouth parish church. Her commander, Pedro de Valdes, fared far better than just about every other senior member of the Armada, most of whom were drowned or disgraced. De Valdes spent three years in comfortable captivity before being ransomed, later he was appointed Governor of Cuba.

20   *Disaster in Ireland*

Up to the middle of September, the Armada's losses had amounted to no more than about 20 ships and perhaps 1,000 men, but in the second half of that month, disaster on an unprecedented scale struck the Spanish fleet, more than doubling its tally of lost ships, and increasing its list of dead six-fold.

Although sixty or more vessels had been able to follow the Duke of Medina Sidonia's instructions to sail well out into the

Atlantic before setting course for Spain, some forty or fifty others were forced, by privation, poor navigation or the continuously foul weather, upon the treacherous coastline of western Ireland. It was there that catastrophe struck, with twenty-six of those ships lost, according to the best contemporary estimates, and about 5,000 men drowned or slaughtered.

Even to those who finally struggled back to Spain, the concluding weeks of the Armada venture must have seemed like some never-ending nightmare, because in addition to the torments of hunger and thirst, especially thirst, and the mounting toll of dead aboard almost every vessel, the storms which raged virtually non-stop were the final ghastly burden. It was as if God was intent of extracting the last ounce of retribution from those Armada crews for their collective sins.

Those storms and the southwesterly gales which accompanied them could not have been a greater handicap to the harried and exhausted remnants of the Spanish fleet, because most of their ships were square-rigged, that is, with square sails rigged in front of the mast, the very worst configuration for confronting adverse winds. In the face of such conditions it would have been difficult and extremely tiring to handle the sails, since the wind would have constantly tended to force them back into the mast, and with the rigging set behind the mast, spilling the wind from a sail would have been a complicated manoeuvre. Thus progress south could have been made only by long, semi-lateral tacks to either wing of the course, broad zig-zags, in other words, a maddeningly slow process for ships in such dire straits.

But slow as it may have been, this method eventually took more than half the Armada home, home to such simple delights as fresh-baked bread, the sight of grapes growing against whitewashed walls, the blessed warmth of the sun, things formerly taken for granted, now acutely savoured.

For most among the thousands shipwrecked in Ireland, however, there was to be nothing but terror and extermination, while even for those few who ultimately escaped, months of fear and deprivation lay ahead.

Given the thick weather the Armada had encountered for most of its journey northwards after the battle of Gravelines, rain, low cloud, fog, weather to make accurate navigation extremely difficult, it seems likely that by the time the Shetlands had been cleared and a westerly course set, few ships' masters would have had much idea precisely where they were. And even those who did, and who deliberately made for Ireland, could not have known the gamble upon which they were embarking. Because Spanish maps of the Irish coast were woefully inaccurate, the most crucial flaw being the total misrepresentation of the county of Mayo, which thrusts itself, a wall of towering cliffs, some forty miles further westwards into the Atlantic than Spanish cartographers of the sixteenth century were aware.

Thus, like flies trapped in an unsuspected web, at least eight south-bound Armada vessels seem to have been lost in the bays of Donegal and Mayo, bays which their captains would not have known existed, and from which they would have been powerless to extricate their cumbersome, unmanoeuvrable ships once caught by the remorseless onshore winds and fierce tides.

It was not on that corner of Ireland's coastline that the first Armada wreck occurred, however, but due north, near the mouth of Lough Foyle. The victim was the *Trinidad Valencera*, that Levanter which earlier had found herself in the company of the *Gran Grifon* and the other two doomed *urcas* somewhere between Orkney and Shetland. After losing touch with them, the *Trinidad* sprang a leak (the fate of so many of the carvel built ships) and for two days her crew pumped non-stop until, in spite of all their efforts, she was wrecked on the coast of Donegal. She thus became one of eight ships from the Levant squadron to be lost – they were just too fragile for those unfamiliar seas, and only two returned to Spain.

The experiences of the 450 or so men who got ashore from the *Trinidad* – about 100 others were drowned – are well documented, and their story is worth recounting since it graphically illustrates the range of horrors which confronted almost all of those from the Armada who survived the initial wrecking of their ships, no matter in what part of Ireland they staggered ashore.

In outlining the apparently treacherous and barbarous conduct of the English troops and their Irish mercenaries, however, it has to be emphasized that the appearance of Spanish ships all along the west of Ireland throughout September of 1588 was an alarming event for Queen Elizabeth's representatives in Dublin. Although they were aware that a Spanish fleet had entered the Channel, they were initially inclined to believe that the vessels now appearing off Ireland were part of a new invasion fleet direct from Spain. And since there were only some 2,000 poorly equipped English soldiers in the whole of Ireland, supported by several thousand Irishmen of doubtful ability and allegiance, the alarm of the authorities was justified. A well-organized force of Spaniards could stir the whole of Catholic Ireland to rebellion, and so it was deemed essential to hunt down the men from the Spanish ships as if they were wild and dangerous animals.

The *Trinidad Valencera* had been wrecked in O'Doherty country, and it was from some of that clan that the Spaniards learned of a Bishop Cornelius living in a castle some four days' march away, and to this they decided to repair.

Upon arriving in the vicinity of the castle, the commander of the *Trinidad*, Colonel Alonzo de Luzon, despatched a messenger to the bishop, asking as one Catholic to another, for help and advice, and as a result was told the castle would be surrendered if his troops made a show of force.

But when de Luzon's men arrived at their destination, someone in the castle fired a cannon, at which, suspecting treason, the Spaniards refused to enter but made instead for a second castle, a ruined building, on the far side of an intervening bog. It was a prudent move because almost at once, English troops were seen approaching, and within a short while the drums of both sides were sounding for a parley. At this meeting the Spaniards asked to be found a ship for Spain, for which they would pay, but were ordered instead to surrender. This they refused to do, saying they would rather die fighting, and despite the threat that 3,000 troops would soon be on hand to cut their throats, they persisted.

For twenty-four hours there was stalemate, then, at night, the queen's men attacked and throughout the hours of darkness, skirmishing ensued. At daylight the Spaniards heard the beat of drums once more and at the subsequent parley, the Irish officer who conducted the negotiations advised them to lay down their arms and allow him to conduct them to Dublin.

With men dying of hunger, and all supplies cut off, Colonel de Luzon agreed to surrender on fair terms of war, providing each of his men was allowed to retain a suit of clothes.

About 350 muskets and a handful of pikes were duly laid down, at which the English force (actually consisting mostly of Irish irregulars, and only 150 strong) promptly fell upon the

Armada men, took everything from them including their clothes, and killed any that resisted.

That night, de Luzon and a handful of senior officers, together with a few friars, were placed inside a square of the queen's troops, while the several hundred other *Trinidad* men were left naked nearby. At dawn next day, these pathetic, frozen creatures were attacked by cavalry and infantry, over 300 being killed, but some 150 managing to escape across the bog to the castle of Bishop Cornelius.

There the many wounded received treatment, and although a number died, most of the survivors of the massacre were eventually spirited from one Catholic household to another across the north of Ireland until, in the McDonnell country of Antrim, they were shipped to Scotland and finally home.

As to those officers and others who were separated from the main body of the Spanish force, they were marched, many still naked, more than 100 miles to imprisonment near Dublin. Some died on that abysmal journey, including the younger brother of Colonel de Luzon; the colonel himself and one other high-ranking Spaniard were despatched to London in the expectation of ransom. Three years later they were still in captivity.

All the rest of that small group were executed, to the disgust of some among the English, who saw the chance of more ransom being wasted.

In 1596, eight Armada men, including two from the *Trinidad Valencera*, were still in Ireland, living under the protection of Hugh O'Neill, Earl of Tyrone, and optimistically petitioning the King of Spain for arrears of pay. They were among a tiny handful of Spaniards who managed to live on in Ireland.

As to the *Trinidad* herself, her remains were discovered in Kinnagoe Bay, Co. Donegal, in 1971, and since then, cannons, broken anchors and much else has been salvaged from her.

On 18 September, four days after the *Trinidad* was wrecked, Sir Richard Bingham, Governor of Connaught, reported seven Spanish ships in the Shannon, not twenty miles from Limerick. Two days later, another correspondent's report showed that number to have grown to twenty-four. From Cork, that same day, Sir John Popham, Attorney General, informed Lord Burghley of Spanish vessels all along the coasts of Clare and Kerry and as far north as Galway Bay.

'The people in these parts are for the most part dangerously affected towards the Spaniards,' he wrote; while Sir Richard Bingham was soon reporting a similar state of affairs to the Lord Deputy of Ireland, Sir William Fytzwylliam. 'The Irishry are grown very proud,' he declared – even his own brother had had his stables burned down and three horses destroyed by local peasants, 'who call themselves the Pope's and King Philip's men.'

It was an alarming situation, and in response to it, orders were issued for the extermination of all Spaniards found in Ireland, while in the West of England and South Wales, troops were commanded to hold themselves at one hour's readiness for service there.

The man principally charged with ensuring the elimination of the Spanish threat was sixty-year-old Sir Richard Bingham, who by one of those quirks of fate common to the age, had served with the Spaniards at the Battle of Lepanto nearly twenty years earlier. Such had been his severity in putting down several clan rebellions in the territory he now governed that he had been awarded the gruesome soubriquet 'the Flail of Connaught'. The starving, half-drowned Spaniards who staggered ashore from their wrecked ships into Bingham's domain were thus doomed from the moment they set foot there – the man and the hour were well met.

On one solitary five-mile stretch of beach, 1,100 corpses were soon to be counted, one Irish irregular claiming to have axed no fewer than eighty men to death in a single orgy of slaughter. With the exception of a few Spanish nobles held for ransom, almost all Armada castaways found in Ireland were executed, old men, boys as young as fourteen, priests, friars, even Dutch and Flemish youths pressed into service against their will.

In the midst of this carnage, a handful did, however, escape, most protected by those Irish chieftains in whose territory the queen's writ could seldom be enforced, but an occasional group chancing upon a humane and compassionate Englishman. One such was Captain Christopher Carlisle, a highly-experienced soldier, and son-in-law of Sir Francis Walsingham, to whom a band of fourteen ragged and starving Spaniards had the good fortune to surrender. Carlisle sent them first to Lord Deputy Fytzwylliam in Dublin, with a letter urging clemency, but they were promptly returned and ordered to be executed. The captain's situation as a relative of one of Queen Elizabeth's most trusted officials enabled him to ignore Fytzwylliam's command; instead, he bought passages on a fishing boat, and after providing the Spaniards with clothing and money, despatched them to Scotland.

In view of the small number of Armada survivors who escaped from Ireland, it is not surprising that little exists in Spanish archives about what happened to those men. One vivid and absorbing account is to be found, however, written by the same Captain de Cuellar who had so narrowly escaped hanging as the Armada was driven northwards in those days after the battle of Gravelines.

Following his reprieve by the Duke of Medina Sidonia, Francisco de Cuellar evidently remained aboard the vessel on which the Judge Advocate had conducted his court martial, another of the Levant squadron, because the latter was drowned before his eyes when their ship and two others were driven ashore by a great gale just south of Donegal Bay.

One thousand men perished on that occasion, among them one of the foremost grandees in the Armada, Don Diego Enriquez, son of the Viceroy of Peru, and commander of the Andalusian squadron.

The manner of the hunchback Don Diego's dramatic death is precisely chronicled by de Cuellar, so that in reading it one almost seems to be witnessing the event.

'Don Diego Enriquez met his death in the most miserable manner that ever was seen,' he reported, 'out of fear of the huge seas which were breaking over the ships, he and the son of the Conde de Villafranca and two other Portuguese gentlemen, carrying with them more than 16,000 ducats worth of jewels and coin, took to the ship's tender, which had a covered deck, and went below, giving orders for the hatch to be battened down and caulked behind them. Thereupon some seventy survivors from the ship threw themselves onto the boat, hoping to reach land in this way, but a great wave overwhelmed and sank her and swept them all away. Afterwards she drifted to and fro in the sea until she was cast ashore, keel upwards, by which misfortune the gentlemen who had taken refuge under the deck died where they were. A day and a half after she had been driven ashore, some savages found the boat, turned her over to get out the nails and iron fittings, and breaking open the hatch, took out the dead men from inside. Don Diego breathed his last in their hands, whereupon they stripped him of his clothes, took all the money and jewels they had with them, and threw the bodies on the ground unburied.'

Captain de Cueller himself was obviously a man born under a lucky star, because having been reprieved after his court martial, he now survived again in circumstances about as terrifying as could be imagined. With the Levanter breaking up fast in mountainous seas, he climbed to the highest point of the tall stern deck, and commending his soul to God, surveyed the appalling scene before him.

'Many were drowning inside their ships,' he later reported, 'others threw themselves into the sea and sank to the bottom, never to reappear, others clutched rafts, barrels or floating timbers, others cried aloud from their ships, imploring God to help them.'

Captains threw their gold neck chains and their money into the sea, he went on, while around them, men were being swept away even from inside their ships.

'I gazed my fill of this fiesta, not knowing what to do, nor what means of escape to try, for I cannot swim and the sea and wind were very great,' he grimly continued. 'Moreover the land and beach were full of enemies dancing and leaping with delight at our misfortunes, and whenever one of us set foot on shore, two hundred savages and other enemies surrounded him and stripped him stark naked, handling him roughly and wounding him without pity.'

At this point, de Cuellar found the Judge Advocate, Martin de Aranda, 'who was very woebegone and miserable', and told him to try and save himself before the ship broke up completely.

The two of them climbed on to a piece of the hull which had broken away, but it was still attached to the ship by iron chains, and so, battered and bruised by the huge seas, and the broken timbers which constantly crashed against them, they got themselves with difficulty on to a hatch door which came swirling by.

But the Judge Advocate was weighed down by the gold coins he had sewn into his doublet and hose, so when another huge wave swept him off the door hatch, he was drowned, crying aloud to God as he sank beneath the sea.

Without de Aranda's weight to balance it, the door began to

turn over, while in the same instant, a baulk of timber crushed de Cuellar's legs. But somehow he managed to hold on, and eventually, covered in blood and too weak to stand, he found himself cast ashore.

Seeing his condition, the Irish plunderers ignored him, so he was able, slowly and painfully, to drag himself away from the beach, passing as he did so many naked Spaniards shivering in the bitter cold. When darkness came he found a deserted spot amid a bed of rushes, and was soon joined by a handsome young man completely naked and in such a state of terror that he was quite unable to speak. A couple of hours later the two were discovered by two men, one carrying a musket, the other a huge axe, but instead of attacking them, the men cut rushes and grass, and without a word, covered them over before heading towards the treasure-strewn beach.

About one in the morning, de Cuellar was awakened from a deep sleep by the noise of a troop of horsemen making for the shore, and when he turned and addressed his companion, he found that he had died. He later learned that he was 'a person of some consequence'.

At daybreak, the captain dragged himself off in search of some monastery where he might get treatment for his injuries, but when he eventually found one, it was deserted, with everything in the church destroyed, and twelve Spaniards hanging from the roof beams.

An old woman hiding her cows in a wood told him the English were in her cottage nearby, so he decided to make for the beach once more in the hope of finding food washed ashore from the wrecks. There he counted more than 400 dead men, including Don Diego Enriquez, who he and two other wounded Spaniards paused to bury.

From then on the resourceful captain, undoubtedly one of life's survivors, experienced an incredible variety of dangers and near disasters in the six months or so he was forced to remain in Ireland. Immediately after burying Don Diego he was badly wounded in the right leg by peasants who stole the gold chain he wore round his neck, and the money hidden in his clothes, but these men later relented and provided him with food, and a poultice for his wound. The next day he was beaten up and stripped naked by Protestant Irish while on his way to the territory in Connaught of Sir Brian O'Rourke, a chieftain who, he had been told, 'was a friend of the King of Spain'. Arriving, after further hazards, in O'Rourke's village, he found some seventy Spaniards already there and the chieftain himself absent, so when he heard of an Armada ship collecting survivors on the nearby coast, he and some twenty others decided to find the ship. But his injured leg hampered progress and it had sailed by the time he got there – which was another stroke of luck since it was soon driven aground, with more than 200 drowned, and others slaughtered.

In great pain from his injuries, half-naked, half-frozen in the bitter autumn weather, de Cuellar was first taken as a virtual slave by some wily blacksmith, then rescued by a local clan chief, with whom he remained, in and out of the mountains of Leitrim for the next three months.

During this time, Lord Deputy Fytzwylliam led a force of 1,700 troops into the west of Ireland to mop up the hundreds of Armada survivors still there, but although Fytzwylliam's men laid seige to the castle where de Cuellar had been given shelter, and although its Irish owner had retreated to the mountains with the rest of his clan, the captain and eight other Spanish fugitives kept the English at bay for nearly three weeks, before heavy snow forced them to turn back towards Dublin.

The lord of the castle was a M'Glannagh, a minor chieftain in O'Rourke's territory, and when he came down from the mountains and found the English gone he was so delighted that he offered de Cuellar one of his sisters in marriage, at the same time, however, making it clear that the Spaniards were too useful as guards to be allowed to leave.

Early next morning, therefore, the captain and four soldiers stole away and began to trek north, intent on reaching the coast and finding a boat for Scotland. The journey took three weeks of January, 1589, and by the time it ended, de Cuellar was on his own once more, his injured leg having caused him to drop behind his companions.

His destination was the castle of Dunluce, stronghold of the McDonnell chieftain who was lord of the route to Scotland, a man who had already given succour to a number of Armada survivors, but when he reached the area he found that boats for Scotland had departed two days earlier. He also discovered, to his dismay, that the district was full of English soldiers.

Totally alone, in great pain from his leg wound, which had

opened up on the long march north, and surrounded by enemies, the captain's plight was about as desperate as at any time since his ship was wrecked, but once again, fortune favoured him. He must have been a personable young man because during his stay with the M'Glannaghs he had clearly charmed the women of the clan, and now his attractiveness came to his aid again, because a group of women took pity on him and led him off to their village in the mountains, where he remained for six weeks while his leg was treated.

At the end of that period he experienced the narrowest escape of his entire saga, because having gone to visit 'some exceedingly beautiful girls', he came face to face with two English soldiers who were also visiting. He was forced to admit his identity, but having extracted a promise from him to accompany them to Dublin, the soldiers turned their attention to the girls, with whom they 'began dallying'. At that point, de Cuellar fled.

Evading the ensuing hue and cry, he eventually reached the castle of the reclusive Bishop of Derry, where he found a dozen other Spaniards. Through the bishop's efforts, a boat was obtained and the party sailed for Scotland, where they were to eke out a miserable six months.

Even after that, Francisco de Cuellar's incredible story does not end, because when, with the Duke of Parma's help, the Armada refugees found boats for Flanders, they were attacked by the Dutch navy and 270 men died. The captain got ashore on a plank of wood, clad in nothing but his shirt; it was almost exactly twelve months from the time of his original shipwreck.

Captain de Cuellar's escape from Ireland was a triumph of fortitude and persistence, but alongside the handful of men who, like him, succeeded in getting away, must be set the many hundreds whose ultimate destiny was the axe or the rope. A number of them probably endured equally perilous experiences and displayed equally admirable heroism, but since fate decreed that they should perish, not one of their stories is known.

Perhaps the most poignant saga of unrewarded resolution concerns the Armada's finest flower, Alonzo de Leyva, commander of the *Rata Coronada*. The *Rata*, another of the ill-fated Levant squadron, ran into Blacksod Bay, Co. Mayo, on 21 September, in company with an Andalusian ship, the *Duquesa Santa Ana*. Blacksod is a two-armed bay, the northern arm, into which the *Santa Ana* sailed, offered one of the safest anchorages in north-west Ireland, the southern one, for which the *Rata* made, more open to the fierce westerlies which roar in off the Atlantic.

The *Rata*'s only remaining anchor had been dropped when she moored, but in the night it began to drag as wind and tide put it to the test, and by daybreak the ship was aground.

(It was lack of adequate anchors which doomed a number of Armada vessels on the wild Irish coast, mainly the result of that fireship raid at Calais, when cables were hacked through and anchors left on the seabed, but partly attributable to the poor quality of Spanish iron, which led to anchors breaking under strain.)

The *Rata* had been anchored within a few hundred yards of a ruined castle, so when she was driven ashore, it was to the castle that her complement of some 500 men repaired. Having fortified it, they then proceeded to burn the *Rata* – her charred remains could still be glimpsed at low tide as late as the beginning of this century – but the Spaniards' location was so desolate, with a huge bog surrounding the castle and stretching endlessly into the distance, that after two days it was decided to make for the other arm of the bay, where the *Duquesa Santa Ana* had taken shelter. It was a difficult march involving tedious detours around swampy inlets, and the crossing of several small rivers, but eventually de Leyva's men reached their destination.

After the Channel battles and ten weeks of strenuous sailing since leaving Corunna, the *Santa Ana* was battered like all the rest of the Armada, but she was patched as well as possible, and the *Rata*'s crew sent aboard to join her own. There were thus some 900 men crammed into her when she got out of Blacksod Bay and set a course for Scotland, but after making 100 miles to the north-east, she too was caught by a storm and driven aground in Loughros More Bay, which lies in the south-west corner of Donegal.

By this time, de Leyva himself was a cripple, having been struck on the leg by a flailing capstan, but he had himself carried ashore and once again proceeded to supervise the transfer ashore of men, arms, food and equipment, and the fortification of yet another ruined castle. The Spaniards were now in M'Sweeney country, from which clan they were able to buy food, and from whom they learned of three other Spanish ships twenty miles to the south in the harbour of Killybegs.

Accordingly, the Spanish force set out to cross the intervening mountains, de Leyva in a litter, and reached Killybegs to discover that only one of the three ships there was in any way seaworthy, she was the *Girona*, one of the four galleasses in the Armada.

The *Girona*'s crew were patching their ship from material salvaged from the other two, and because she had the rudder problems common to all the galleasses, they were having to rig up another. Like all of her type, she was a big ship, with nearly 300 mariners and soldiers and about as many galley slaves, so that by the time de Leyva's men arrived, the village of Killybegs must have had more than 1,600 men overwhelming it.

Big as she was, there was no possibility of the *Girona* carrying that number, so about 300 men, including a number of Irish together with many sick and wounded were left behind, and on 26 October, Alonzo de Leyva once more gave the order to sail.

Doggedly the heavily-overloaded ship made her way northwards on a southwesterly wind, and the weather was so good for a while that the chief pilot, seeing the wind shift to the north, calculated that, rather than make for Scotland, they could reach Spain in five days. For a while, optimism must have run high, but it was as false as fool's gold because that night the northerly wind increased to a gale, and without an effective rudder, and despite the efforts of the galley-slaves, the *Girona* was forced further and further inshore until, in pitch darkness and a huge sea, she was dashed against a reef close to the Giant's Causeway on the north shore of Co. Antrim.

All but nine men were drowned, the magnificent Alonzo de Leyva, all the golden lads from Spain's greatest houses, all their retinues of servants, all, down to the humblest, most despised galley slave were engulfed.

Throughout the voyage from Spain, de Leyva had carried with him secret instructions which empowered him to take over command of the Armada in the event of disaster overtaking Medina Sidonia; for King Philip, like almost every other Spaniard, he was the glittering epitome of that particular blend of bravery and chivalry which the whole nation revered.

The Armada disaster turned the king's beard white, but his deepest grief was said to have been the death of that one man.

The site of the *Girona*'s wreck, off a point still known as

Spaniard's Rock, was discovered in 1968, and many of the jewels and gold chains worn by those peacock-proud grandees of the Spanish fleet were recovered. Perhaps the saddest find was a gold ring, with the simple message in Spanish, 'I have no more to give thee'.

21   *Prisoners and Fugitives*

It was not until the end of August that the English authorities felt sufficiently confident about the defeat of the Armada to anounce it publicly, the pronouncement being entrusted to the Dean of St Paul's Cathedral.

This was the time when those who had actually achieved the victory, Lord Howard, Sir Francis Drake and their fellow commanders, were still on duty, grappling with the problems of sick and unpaid seamen, and tired ships, so that, in London, the stage was clear for such peripheral figures as the Earl of Leicester to bask in the limelight of public rejoicing.

After the break-up of the Tilbury camp, Leicester returned in the manner of a conqueror, parading through the city with a large retinue of gentlemen 'as if he were a king', in the words of a Spanish spy. This must have been the earl's last public appearance, however, because a few days later he died, while on his way to his castle at Kenilworth.

Not long after Leicester's death, Londoners had been offered a fascinating spectacle, eleven captured Armada banners suspended from the battlements of old St Paul's, and they were still in place when, on 24 November, Queen Elizabeth attended the cathedral in great state for a service of thanksgiving.

The huge wave of relief which swept across the nation when news of the Armada's defeat was known, may be sensed by the number of bequests left for the special purpose of commemorating the event. As late as the end of the last century, 300 years on, sermons were still being preached in consequence of such bequests.

Towards the end of October, 1588, a ship was wrecked in Hope Cove, near Salcombe, Devon; she was, improbably, an Armada vessel, the *San Pedro el Mayor*, from the *urca* squadron. She was, in fact, not strictly an *urca*, but one of two hospital ships which had accompanied the Spanish fleet, and why she fetched up on the Devonshire coast nearly three months after passing that way with the Armada, is a mystery.

She evidently sailed well west of Ireland, as decreed by the Duke of Medina Sidonia, but then instead of continuing on a southwesterly course for Spain, somehow turned due east, thus completing a full circuit of England, Scotland and Ireland. Whether her end was simply a matter of stormy weather, or was partly attributable to the notorious wiles of the wreckers of that area, will never be known. What is known is that about forty of her crew were drowned when she struck the rocks, and a hundred or more got ashore. The survivors seem to have been in far better condition than were most other members of the Spanish fleet who lived to tell the sorry tale, which was perhaps not surprising since, as a medical ship, she would have been better provisioned than most other Armada vessels.

It took several days for news of the *San Pedro* to filter through to the authorities from that remote spot where she had sunk, and by the time the fact was known, both ship and survivors had been well plundered by the local populace. When the Deputy Lieutenant of Devon, George Cary, reached Hope Cove from his home at Cockington, he discovered that about 6,000 ducats worth of medical supplies had been stolen or ruined by sea water, and that the crew had been relieved of all their money and valuables.

'There are no persons of account in the ship,' he reported to the Privy Council, only 'soldiers and such as have risen by service, and bestowed all their wealth in this action.'

None the less, about a dozen men were separated from the rest and imprisoned in the charge of Sir William Courteney, a local dignitary. They were the unfortunate ones, because whereas most of the remainder were released for small ransoms after about a year, Courteney kept his prisoners until the end of 1591, continually raising his ransom demands.

Some two or three miles from Hope Cove is the Thurlestone Inn, and there are to be found ceiling beams made from the timbers of the *San Pedro*; and after a northeasterly blow, when the under surface of inner Hope beach is exposed, coins bearing the Spanish royal arms are still to be occasionally discovered.

The defeat of the Armada had extinguished in England whatever hopes Catholics might have entertained for the resurgence of their faith, but in Scotland, where increasing numbers of Spanish fugitives were arriving, the Catholic nobility were far more active, and thus the presence there of a growing force of Spaniards was a matter to be carefully monitored by the English authorities.

It had been a common belief among Armada survivors that once in Scotland, their troubles would be over, that King James would shelter them, clothe them, and find them passages for Spain, but upon arrival they were quickly disabused of that idea. Captain de Cuellar discovered the reality of the situation soon after he set foot on Scottish soil; far from favouring the Spaniards, he complained, the king was good to none of them. 'Nor did he give a single real out of charity, and all those of us who came to his kingdom suffered the greatest privations.'

For all the cool treatment meted out by the monarch, the fact remained that a hard core of Scottish nobles, led by men like the earls of Bothwell, Huntly and Montrose, had been in subversive contact with Spain for years, so when reports began to reach London that in addition to fugitive Spaniards, an Armada ship had also arrived in Scotland, there was cause for some concern.

It was towards the end of September that the *San Juan de Sicilia* sailed into the bay of Tobermory, the port in the far north of the Isle of Mull, 'beaten with shot and weather', according to William Asheby, the English ambassador to Scotland.

Asheby's report, which found its way to Sir Francis Walsingham, as head of the Secret Service, spoke of some 800 men aboard, although the ship's original complement had been about 350, but whatever the figure, Walsingham obviously decided that the threat posed by the *San Juan* and her crew should be decisively countered. And as with so many of the Secretary's projects, it was triumphantly achieved.

Tobermory was part of the territory of the fearsome McLane clan, and the arrival there of the Armada ship was greeted with pleasure by the clan chieftain, Lauchlan McLane, since it meant that a windfall force of men and weapons were suddenly available to reinforce the band of thugs who formed his own private army. Accordingly he 'borrowed' two canon and 100 men from the Spaniards and proceeded to terrorize the nearby islands of Muck, Eig and Rhum, and the adjacent mainland district of Ardnamurchan.

Meanwhile, the rest of the *San Juan de Sicilia*'s crew, commanded by 'a person of great account', in the words of the English ambassador, but never positively identified by historians, were able to exist in comparative comfort since they had sufficient funds to pay for everything they acquired, a fact which favourably impressed the natives of those western isles.

Among those who grew friendly with the Spaniards during the five or six weeks they were at Tobermory was a certain John Smollett (an ancestor of the author Tobias Smollett) who was eventually left free to wander wherever he wished aboard the *San Juan*. It was a fatal friendship for those Armada survivors, because Smollett was an agent of Walsingham.

On 18 November, a certain Roger Aston reported from Edinburgh to his brother, 'This day, word is come that the great ship which lay in the west isles is blown in the air by device of John Smollett, most part of the men are slain.'

What happened, Aston went on, was that Smollett, 'a man that has great trust among the Spaniards, entered the ship and cast in the powder room a piece of lint, and so departed. A short time after, the lint took fire and burnt ship and men.'

According to Captain Charles Eggerton, writing to Lord Deputy Fytzwylliam in Dublin, a Scottish merchant reported that around 700 men had been killed in the explosion, including five Scots left as hostages by Lauchlan McLane for the 100 Spaniards recruited to his army. The chieftain's own foster son had been one of the hostages. Only two or three men survived the carnage, having been blown ashore from the upper deck when the ship exploded.

In July 1589, the *San Juan* survivors, including half the force serving with McLane, were put aboard ships with other Armada refugees and despatched to Flanders. A storm forced the flotilla to seek shelter in English ports, but by then the English authorities had had their fill of Spanish prisoners of war, and so allowed the ships to proceed unmolested once the weather improved.

According to the English ambassador, Lauchlan McLane refused to allow the other fifty Spaniards in his private army to leave, while elsewhere in Scotland small groups of Armada survivors stayed on of their own free will, 'sparkled abroad in noblemen's houses, choosing rather to lead a serving man's life at ease in this country than to follow the wars in Flanders in want and danger.'

Of the 30,000 men who set out from Lisbon with the Armada, only a minute handful lingered on in either Scotland or Ireland, so the 400-year-old legend that whole colonies of Spaniards settled, thrived and stamped their features on those two nations has no foundation in fact.

As to the *San Juan de Sicilia*, like so many other ships which sailed in that Spanish fleet, she was reputed to have been rich with treasure, and for more than 250 years, since the early 1700s, in fact, spasmodic attempts have been made to discover it.

Early one morning in December of 1588, the Reverend James Melville, one of the foremost citizens of the Scottish port of Anstruther, in the county of Fife, was roused from his bed by the town baillie, who reported that a force of Spaniards had come ashore, 'not to give mercy, but to ask.'

They were, it transpired, the crew of the *Gran Grifon*, flagship of the *urca* squadron, the vessel wrecked on Fair Isle some three months previously.

The baillie had ordered them back to their ship, and now desired the Reverend Melville to hear their petition, which he shortly prepared to do by gathering a quorum of Anstruther's notables.

'There presents to us a man of big stature and grave and stout countenance,' Melville recorded in his diary, 'grey-haired and very humble-like, who after many low curtsies, bowing down his face near the ground, and touching my shoe with his hand, began his harangue in the Spanish tongue.'

It was Juan Gomez de Medina, commander of the squadron of *urcas*, one of the most senior officers in the Armada.

As a result of Medina's servile plea for assistance, he and five fellow officers were allowed to stay on shore, but it was not until the following day that the Laird of Anstruther gave permission for the remaining 260 men to leave ship. These were, Melville recorded, 'for the most part young, beardless men, feeble, dragging their limbs after them with debility.'

The Scots found food for these 'silly, trauchled and hungered' youths, but even as the Spaniards wolfed down the kail, porridge and fish which had been provided, James Melville could not help contemplating how Spaniards might have treated non-Catholic Scots had they landed in Spain in similar circumstances.

The crew of the *Gran Grifon* had spent a month on Fair Isle after their shipwreck, devouring everything in sight, before finding a boat for Shetland. At their departure they left fifty of their fellows buried at a spot still known as Spanniarts Graves.

By the time they found another boat to carry them to the Scottish mainland they had lived in semi-isolation for three months, and thus knew nothing of the disasters which had overtaken the Armada, and confidently imagined the fleet safely back in home ports. But one day, on a visit to the ancient university city of St Andrews, James Melville got hold of a news-sheet giving details of wrecked ships, and the names of some of the principal Armada officers who had died.

When the information was read to Juan Gomez de Medina, he burst into tears.

The *Gran Grifon*'s crew were soon shipped on to Edinburgh, where they remained until joining the ships for Flanders, eight months later.

For the citizens of Anstruther, 'it had been a good Christian act they had performed, but there must have been many there who, like James Melville, gave thanks to God that the Spaniards had come to their town as supplicants, rather than conquerors.'

22   *End of a Flawed Enterprise*

The nightmare voyage home ended for most of the surviving Armada ships in the last days of September, by which time the majority had been continuously at sea for three months, and sailed some 5,000 miles. Nobody knows the precise number that got back to Spain, although a figure of seventy is probably fairly accurate, but after so long abroad and in such hostile seas, many were only good for the breaker's yard. Indeed, it was a miracle, in the view of one observer, that they stayed afloat long enough to get home at all.

The *San Martin*, the Duke of Medina Sidonia's flagship, reached the Biscayan port of Santander on 21 September; of her crew, 180 were dead from disease and starvation, and 40 more had been killed in battle. The remainder were so weak they could not work the ship into port and she had to be taken in tow.

The duke himself had been ill with fever and dysentery for nearly a month, semi-conscious for much of the time, his will sapped and his hair turned grey by sickness and adversity. Of his personal retinue of sixty, all but two were dead or seriously ill.

According to the Venetian ambassador, twenty-four ships eventually reached Santander, all in a bad way, and one having lost every single man to ravaging disease by the time it had been a few days in port.

Such had been conditions at the end of the voyage that some ships had not had a drop of drinking water for two weeks, the only relief to tormenting thirst coming when crews wrung rainwater from their shreds of clothes.

Despite the illness which continued to prostrate him, leaving him too weak at times even to sign his name, Medina Sidonia struggled on ashore with a makeshift staff for nearly three weeks before King Philip released him from his duties; he had vowed never to accept command at sea again, even if it cost him his head, but, like Lord Howard, he could not lightly relinquish responsibility for the men who had endured so much and served so gallantly under his command.

Accordingly, a series of urgent appeals went forth from his temporary headquarters at Santander, to the king, to the Archbishop of Burgos, and to the governor of the province, calling for fresh supplies of food and medicine, money for unpaid men, and adequate care for the multitude of sick.

Unlike Queen Elizabeth, the Spanish king seems to have shown considerable concern for the sufferings of his Armada forces, and once a degree of organization had been established, the care they received was as good as could have been expected in the unpromising circumstances.

None the less, with so many sick, it was a daunting task which confronted the authorities, as a local official reported to the Secretary of the War Council. There were over 1,000 men in Santander alone in urgent need of treament, he declared. 'If they are brought ashore, the hospital would be so overcrowded that the infection would spread, and if they are left to sleep in the stench and wretchedness of the ships, the fit are bound to fall ill. It is impossible to attend to so many.'

For all that, a month later the Venetian ambassador was able to report that all the soldiers returning with the Armada had been found lodgings, but, he added, 'They do not amount to 5,000 out of the 18,000 and upwards which embarked, and they are all in a very bad way.'

By the time of that report, the Duke of Medina Sidonia had been carried the length of Spain in a curtained horse-litter to his estate near Cadiz. The journey took a month, and the small convoy transporting the duke and his few retainers travelled as inconspicuously as possible, avoiding the great houses and large cities along its 500-mile route, because most people blamed him for the Armada's failure.

The large number of ships which had failed to return had sent a profound shock throughout the Spanish nation, hardly a family had not been touched in one way or another by the extent of the tragedy, and the fleet's commander was thus an obvious target for condemnation.

'What is heard on all sides is the bad generalship and timidity of the Duke of Medina Sidonia,' an observer declared, 'everyone lays the blame of all these misfortunes upon his inexperience and lack of valour.'

Not everyone, King Philip, for one, apportioned no direct blame for the Armada's defeat, although he did imprison the duke's naval adviser, Diego Flores de Valdes, for fifteen months. The taciturn Diego Flores had been in an impossible position in trying to combat the tactics of the English fleet, but this had not been appreciated by some of the most senior military men aboard the Spanish ships, who doubtless made their dissatisfaction widely known on returning to Spain. Furthermore, he had abandoned the *Rosario*, the ship of his cousin,

Pedro de Valdes, on that first day of conflict in the Channel, and Pedro had been quick to get his version of events to the king. If Philip's frustration demanded at least one scapegoat, then Diego Flores was a ready-made victim.

For the Duke of Medina Sidonia, the public contumely heaped upon him was bad enough, based as it was upon ignorance and spite, but almost as distressing to him must have been the fact that despite his original protestation to the king that he was too much in debt to accept command of the Armada, by the time he got back to his estate in Andalusia he had been driven thousands of reals deeper into debt by the enterprise.

Whatever the Spanish nation might think of the duke's performance, however, to many in the Armada it was the Duke of Parma who was the principal culprit, but here, too, the king would not hear a word of condemnation. By the end of 1588 he was discussing the possibility of the duke returning secretly to Spain to organize a new attempt against England, and to demonstrate his faith in Parma, he sacked one of his most outspoken critics, the Armada's Inspector General, Don Jorge Manrique, who had originally clashed with the duke over the unreadiness of his invasion preparations at Dunkirk and Nieuport.

But considerately as King Philip treated Medina Sidonia, the mark of failure remained etched upon his features for the rest of his life. Even his own servants sometimes spoke against him in private, fervently as they might publicly defend his name.

None the less, for over two decades the duke continued to hold high office, for ten years under Philip, the remainder in the service of his successor.

Others were less fortunate. The gallant Miguel de Oquendo, commander of the Guipuzcoan squadron, nursed his ship all the way back to San Sebastian, then, refusing to meet a single member of his family, turned his face to the wall and expired of exhaustion and despair. A few days later, the ship's magazine exploded, killing a hundred of the surviving crew.

The even more gallant Juan de Recalde, admiral of the squadron of Biscayans, also died upon reaching port. At the age of sixty-two, he had performed feats of which a thirty-year old would have been proud, but he had been ill throughout the voyage home, like so many others. By the time his ship, the *San*

Juan, reached Spanish waters in early October, 170 men were already dead, and the daily ration of food had been reduced to a mere four ounces of biscuit.

Recalde's vessel had been one of the few to have avoided disaster on the coast of Ireland, having sheltered at the mouth of Dingle Bay, in Co. Kerry, for thirteen days while the crew took on fresh water and waited for the weather to clear. The *San Juan* had been accompanied into the bay by the vice flagship of the Castile squadron, the *San Juan de Bautista*, and while there the crews of the two vessels had watched a third Armada ship, a big converted merchantman, come flying in in a great storm, drag her anchor and sink, with the loss of all but one man.

With Armada ships limping home throughout late September and on into October, officials on shore were striving to forge some order amid the chaos of sick and starving men, broken ships and rotting foodstuffs. Despite precautions, many of those even half-fit were deserting at the first opportunity, but most of the returnees, cursed for weeks with stinking water and uneatable food, were simply too feeble to stir. According to an English spy, several of the principal provisioning officers were executed when the full extent of the fleet's suffering became known, but by then it was the sorry state of the ships, as much as the men, which was causing anxiety. Because with King Philip already talking of another attempt against England, new ships were much harder to come by than new men.

If another fleet was to be assembled quickly, the Secretary of the War Council was informed by an official in Santander, there was nothing for it but for that worthy himself to come and take charge of affairs.

'If you cannot come at once,' the official wrote, 'I shall look upon the Armada as in abeyance until the year '90. I am bound to think that the year of the eights, so ardently looked forward to, will turn out to be 1800.'

Throughout Europe, 1588 had been predicted as a momentous year, and for Spain, an auspicious one. In fact, of course, events were to prove that no year was a favourable one for Spanish operations against England. In 1596 a fleet set out for Ireland, but it was the beginning of winter, and it was storm-wrecked even before it had left home waters. The next year another force was despatched, this one aiming to seize Falmouth and establish itself in Cornwall. It too was thwarted by the weather.

The disaster of 1588 cost Spain some sixty ships and up to 20,000 men, including the deaths of five of the dozen most senior commanders, and the detention of two others, but although it left King Philip visibly aged, and more reclusive than ever, it did little to subdue his determination.

God was to be thanked, he averred, that another fleet as powerful as the Armada could be assembled – the stream might be temporarily choked, but the source flowed freely.

Even the country's ever more critical financial position would not be allowed to stand in the way. 'We will sell these candle-sticks if no other way of raising money can be found,' he declared defiantly as he and his advisers conferred around a candle-lit table.

But did Philip, in moments of deepest reflection, ever consider his own responsibility for the failure of the Armada? Because if any one man could be blamed for the disaster it was surely the king himself; with no more than theoretical knowledge of war, or of the conditions his men were likely to encounter, and with only the most skeletal intelligence concerning the capabilities of the English fleet, he it was who mapped out the grand design, whose daily attention to detail even extended to the amount of water the men of the Armada should take with their wine.

To the Spanish nation, the fleet's humiliation was a consequence of foul weather and Medina Sidonia's timidity. To the king the reason was more complex, and at the same time, more simple. It was the will of God, no one could gainsay the will of God, it was pointless to pursue the matter further.

Bibliography

Calendar of the Carew Manuscripts, ed. J.S. Brewer & W. Bullen (Lambeth Library, London)
Calendar of State Papers, Domestic (1581-90), ed. R. Lemon (HMSO 1865)
Calendar of State Papers, Foreign (Jan-June 1588), vol. xxi, pt. iv, ed. S.C. Lomas & A.B. Hines (HMSO, London, 1931)
Calendar of State Papers, Irish (1586-88), ed. H.C. Hamilton (Longman & Co, London, 1877)
Calendar of State Papers, Venetian (1581-91), ed. H.F. Brown (Eyre & Spottiswoode, London, 1894)
Calendar of Letters & Papers relating to English Affairs preserved in the archives of Simancas, (1587-1603), vol. iv, ed. M.A.S. Hume (Eyre & Spottiswoode, London 1899)
Harleian Miscellany, T. Osborne (London, 1753)
Musters, Beacons, Subsidies etc., in the County of Northants 1586-1623, ed. J. Wake (Northants Record Society, Kettering, 1926)
Naval Tracts: vol. 1, W. Monson (Navy Records Society, 1894)
Report on arrangements when Spain projected the invasion and conquest of England, J. Bruce (1798)
Spanish Armada Documents, Naval Miscellany vol. IV, ed. G.P.B. Naish, (Navy Records Society, 1952)
State Papers Relating to the Defeat of the Spanish Armada, ed. J.K. Laughton (Navy Records Society, 1894)

Aikin, L., Memoirs of the Court of Queen Elizabeth, vol. 2 (Longman, London, 1822)
Beckingsale, B.W., Burghley (Macmillan, London, 1967)
Boynton, L., The Elizabethan Militia: 1558-1638 (Routledge Kegan Paul, London, 1967)
Callendar, G., The Naval Side of British History (Christophers, London, 1924)
Cary, R., Memoirs of Robert Cary (John Murray, London, 1808)
Clarke, G.S. & Thursfield, T.R., The Navy and the Nation (John Murray, London, 1897)
Corbett, J.S., Drake and the Tudor Navy, vol. 2 (Longmans Green, London, 1898)
Cruikshank, C.G., Elizabeth's Army (Clarendon Press, Oxford, 1966)
Dietz, F.C., English Public Finance, 1558-1641 (pp. xviii, 478, American Historical Association, 1932)
Duro, C.F., La Armada Invencible (Madrid, 1884)

Fallon, N., *The Armada in Ireland* (Stanford Maritime, London, 1978)
Fortescue, J.W., *History of the British Army* (Macmillan, London 1910)
Froude, J.A., *Spanish Story of the Armada* (Longman, London, 1892)
Froude, J.A., *English Seamen in the 16th Century* (Longman, London, 1895)
Graham, W., *The Spanish Armada* (Collins, London, 1972)
Green, E., *Somerset and the Armada* (Harrison & Sons, London, 1888)
Hadfield, A.M., *Time to Finish the Game* (Phoenix House, London, 1964)
Hardie, R.P., *Tobermory Argosy* (Oliver & Boyd, Edinburgh, London, 1912)
Hardy, E., *Survivors of the Armada* (Constable, London, 1966)
Howarth, D., *The Voyage of the Armada* (Penguin, London, 1982)
Lloyd, C.C., *British Seamen 1200-1860* (Collins, London, 1968)
Martin, C., *Full Fathom Five* (Chatto & Windus, London, 1975)
Mattingley, G., *The Defeat of the Spanish Armada* (Jonathan Cape, London, 1959)
Melvill, J., *The Autobiography and Diary of Mr James Melvill*, ed. R. Pitcairn (Woodrow Society, Edinburgh, 1842)
Noble, T.C., *Rise and Fall of the Spanish Armada* (Russell Smith, London, 1886)
Noble, W.M., *Huntingdonshire and the Spanish Armada* (E. Stock, London, 1896)
Predmore, R.L., *Cervantes* (Thames and Hudson, London, 1973)
Read, C., *Mr Secretary Walsingham*, vols. 1 & 2 (Clarendon Press, Oxford, 1925)
Rowse, A.L., *The Expansion of Elizabethan England* (Macmillan, London, 1955)
Straker, E., *Wealden Iron* (G. Bell & Sons, London, 1931)
Tenison, E.M., *Elizabethan England: vol. VII*, 13 vols. (Royal Leamington Spa, 1933-60)
Williamson, J.A., *The Age of Drake* (Collins, London, 1951)
Williamson, J.A., *Hawkins of Plymouth* (Adam & Charles Black, London, 1969)
Woodrooffe, T., *Vantage at Sea* (St Martin's Press, New York, 1958)
Wright, T., *Elizabeth and Her Times: vol. 2* (Henry Colburn, London, 1838)

Bovill, E.W., 'Queen Elizabeth's gunpowder', *Mariner's Mirror*, vol. 33, 1947, University Press, Cambridge
Christy, M., 'Queen Elizabeth's visit to Tilbury, 1588', *English History Review*, vol. 34, Jan-Oct 1919, Longmans Green & Co, London
Glasgow, T. jun., 'The shape of ships that defeated the Spanish Armada', *Mariner's Mirror*, vol. 50, 1964, University Press, Cambridge
Lewis, M., 'Armada guns', *Mariner's Mirror*, vol. 29, 1943, University Press, Cambridge
Thompson, I.A.A., 'Appointment of Duke of Medina Sidonia', *Historical Journal*, vol. 12, 1970, University Press, Cambridge
Waters, D.W., 'Elizabethan Navy and Armada', *Mariner's Mirror*, vol. 35, 1949, University Press, Cambridge

Index

Abingdon, 17
Aldeburgh, 40
Allen, Cardinal, 35, 103
Andalucia, 10, 22
Anstruther, 149, 150
Antrim, 136
de Aranda, Martin, 139
Arceo, Secretary, 84, 87
Armada: sails, 10; at Corunna, 18*f*; Lisbon chaos, 22; water problems, 23; leaves Corunna, 44; King Philip's instructions, 46; Biscay storm, 48; first skirmish, 53*f*; first losses, 59*f*; Portland Bill battle, 61*f*; Isle of Wight battle, 75*f*; Calais anchorage, 84; fireships, 89; Gravelines battle, 94*f*; the Zeeland banks, 100*f*; retreat northwards, 119*f*; wrecks in Ireland, 132*f*; prisoners, 145; homecoming, 150*f*
Ark Royal, 42, 62, 64, 65, 68, 70, 78, 82, 91
Ascoli, Prince of, 109
Asheby, W., 147-9
Aubrey, J., 10
de Avila, C., 121-2

Barca de Amburg, 123
Bark Buggins, 77
barrel staves, 23
Bath, 17
beacons, 34, 35
Berry Head, 61, 64
de Bertendona, M., 67
Bingham, Sir R., 136, 137
Biscay, Bay of, 43, 48
Blacksod Bay, 142
Blakeney, 40
de Bobadilla, Gen., 122
Boleyn, Anne, 27
Bond, M., 118
Borlas, W., 98
Bridewell Prison, 130
Bruges, 111
Burghley, Lord, 15, 32, 36, 38, 39, 71, 72, 113, 117, 127-9
Burgos, Archbishop of, 151

Cadiz, 22
Calais, 84, 86, 90
Calderon, P., 122, 123, 138
Cambridge, 17
Cape Clear, 27
Carey, Sir G., 31, 80
Carlisle, Capt. C., 137

Cary, G., 130-2, 146
Cary, R., 34, 70, 75, 112
Castilla Negro, 123
Castro de Rio, 9
de Cervantes, M., 9
Chichester, 17
Clare, 136
Cley, 40
Clowes, W., 42
Columbell, R., 15
Conception de Zubelzu, 77
Corunna, 18-25, 52
Courteney, Sir W., 146
Croft, Sir J., 25
Cromwell, Sir H., 34, 35
Crosse, R., 102
de Cuellar, Capt. F., 121, 122, 138-42, 147
Cumberland, Earl of, 70, 75, 112, 119

Darley Hall, Derbyshire, 15, 16
Derry, Bishop of, 142
Disdain, 53, 55
Donegal, 123, 134, 136
Dorset, 16, 65, 116
Dover, 31
Drake, Sir F., 13-15, 23-9, 42, 43, 49, 53, 57, 62-4, 68, 71, 76-9, 90, 94, 104, 107, 127, 145
Dunkirk, 23, 83, 84, 93, 109, 112
Dunwich, 40
Duquesta Santa Ana, 142-3

East Bergholt, 40
Eddystone, 52
Eggerton, Capt. C., 148
Elizabeth the First, 25-7, 36, 38, 43, 71, 83, 84, 112, 113-18, 126-9
Elizabeth Bonaventure, 70
Elizabeth Jonas, 56, 57, 79, 127
Enriques, Don D., 138-40
Exeter, 40
Exmouth, 40

Fair Isle, 124, 150
Fenner, T., 49-51, 65
fireships, 89, 93
Flanders, 20, 73-5, 142, 148
Fleming T., 49-51, 65
Flushing, 74
Fowey, 51-2
Frob˙sher, 27, 57, 63, 68, 71, 77, 78, 82, 94
Fytzwylliam, Sir W., 137, 141

Galway Bay, 136
German prisoners, 131
Geronimo, Padre, 100
Giambelli, F., 89
Giant's Causeway, 144
Girona, 144
Golden Hind, 14, 49, 51, 65
Golden Lion, 78
de Gourdan, M., 85, 92
Gran Grifon, 76, 123, 124, 134, 149, 150
Gran Grin, El, 57
Gravelines, Battle of, 95-100
Great St Helen's Church, 118
gunpowder, 30
guns & gunnery, 28, 29, 99

Hatfield House, 117
Hatton, Sir C., 16
Harwich, 32
Hawkins J., 15, 27, 37, 41, 42, 57, 64, 67, 71, 76, 77, 79, 82, 85, 94, 102
Heredia, Capt. P., 85
Hereford, 17
Hobbes, T., 10
Hogge, R., 29
Hope, 41, 98, 102
Hope Cove, 146
Howard, Lord, 26, 27, 32, 37-41, 51, 53, 55-7, 62, 66-9, 75, 76, 81-3, 87, 92, 95, 103, 104, 113, 126, 145
Howard, Lord Thomas, 64, 78
Hunsdon, Lord, 116

Ipswich, 42
Irish mercenaries, 134, 135
Isle of Wight, 31, 50, 80, 81

Justin, Count of Nassau, 74, 111

Kerry, 136
Killybegs, 144
Kinnagoe Bay, 136
King's Lynn, 40
Kingston upon Hull, 40

Lancashire, 17
La Rambla, 9
Lee, G., 45
Leicester, Earl of, 72, 113-18, 145
Leigh, R., 36
de Leon, Capt., 81
Lepanto, 9, 56, 103, 137
Levantine squadron, 10, 99, 105, 123
de Leyva, A., 50, 56, 64, 66, 68, 101, 142-5
Limburger, H., 10, 18, 30
Lisbon, 9, 20, 22
Liverpool, 17
Lizard Beacon, 50
London, 17
losses (men), 99
Lough Foyle, 134
Loughross More Bay, 143

de Luzon, Col. A., 135, 136
Lyme Bay, 65
Lyme Regis, 40

McDonnell, 136, 141
M'Glannagh, 141, 142
McLane, L., 148, 149
M'Sweeney, 143
Makeshift, 77
Manrique, Jorge, 86, 110, 153
Manrique, Juan, 110
Margaret and John, 60, 61, 63, 91
Margate, 126, 127
Maria Juan, 98
Mary, Queen of Scots, 13
Mary Rose, 62
Mayo, 134, 142
de Medina, J., 149, 150
Medina Sidonia, Duke of, 11, 19, 20, 21, 23, 24, 27, 44-7, 50, 53, 55, 57-9, 64-8, 72, 77, 82, 87, 93, 110, 122, 124, 151-5
Melville, Revd J., 149, 150
de Mendoza, B., 36, 103, 106, 108, 109
Milford Haven, 32
Militia: unpreparedness, 16f; pay, 18; training, 32; retreat policy, 33; Tilbury assembly, 112-18
de Miranda, Don L., 101
de Moncada, H., 65-7, 90
Montagu, Lord, 98
Montgomery, Gen., 33
Moonshine, 77
Morocco, 30
Morosini Capt. F., 73
Mulsho, Sir J., 115

Navy, English: new style ships, 28; expert gunners, 29; victualling problems, 38; fear of sickness, 41; returns to Plymouth, 43; sights Armada, 52; new tactics, 56; Portland Bill battle, 61-9; Isle of Wight battle, 75-81; Calais fireships, 89, 90; Gravelines battle, 93-100; death & disease, 127-9; homecoming, 126-9
Nelson, Adm., 43
Newcastle, 108
Nieuport, 83, 111
Nonpareil, 67, 94
Norris, Sir J., 72, 114
Northumberland, Earl of, 34, 99
Nuestra Senora del Barrio, 77
Nuestra Senora del Rosario, 58, 60, 61, 63, 91, 130-2

Ochoa, D., 82
d'Olivares, Count, 106
O'Neill, H., 136
de Oquendo, M., 65, 101, 153
Orford, 40
Orkneys, 127
Ormonde, Earl of, 117
O'Rourke, Sir B., 140

Owers, the, 80
Oxford, 17

Palavicino, Sir H., 70, 95
Panama Isthmus, 14
Parma, Duke of: 11, 13, 19, 20, 23, 25, 46, 50,
    51, 66, 72, 74, 77, 83, 84, 86, 87, 109,
    111, 112, 118, 153
Philip the Second, King of Spain, 9, 19, 20, 22,
    24, 37, 45, 47, 48, 50, 51, 59, 74, 83,
    107-9, 124, 144, 151-5
Pimentel, Don D., 97
Plymouth, 10, 14, 26, 39, 43, 50-2, 61
Poole, 40
Pope Sixtus the Fifth, 24, 84, 106
Popham, Sir J., 136
Portland Bill, 61-9
Portsdown Beacon, 35
Portsmouth, 31, 70
Portugal, 20, 47
Preston, A., 91

Raleigh, Sir W., 29, 104
Rame Head, 52, 55
Rata Coronada, 56, 57, 67, 78, 142, 143
de Recalde, Juan, 50, 56, 57, 69, 96, 101, 153
Regazona, 67
Revenge, 57, 62, 94
Roebuck, 62
Rouen correspondent, 107

St Paul's Cathedral, 145
San Christobal, 48, 60
San Felipe, 77, 96, 98, 125
San Juan de Portugal, 56, 57, 64, 68, 79, 80
San Juan de Sicilea, 147, 148
San Lorenzo, 90, 92, 93
San Luis, 77, 78
San Marcos, 77, 93, 105
San Martin, 44, 47, 49, 55, 58-60, 67-9, 77-9,
    85, 87, 90, 93-5, 97, 101, 105, 109, 125,
    151
San Mateo, 77, 79, 80, 96-8, 125
San Pedro, 121
San Pedro el Mayor, 146, 147
San Salvador, 58, 64, 130, 131
Santa Anna, Andalusian Squadron, 78
Santa Anna, Biscay Flagship, 49
Santa Barbara, 121
Santa Cruz, Marquis of, 21, 22, 25, 26, 46
Santander, 151, 152
Scilly Isles, 37, 49
Scotland, 137, 143, 147-150
Serrano, Capt. A., 88, 89

Seymour, Lord Henry, 51, 70, 72, 81, 83,
    85, 87, 96, 102
Shetlands, 119, 134, 150
Sidmouth, 40
Smollett, J., 148, 149
Southampton, 40, 119
Southwell, Sir R., 67
Spanish prisoners, 129-32
Stafford, Sir E., 108
Studland Bay, 40, 131
Sussex, Earl of, 31

Tagus, River, 10, 19
Teignmouth, 40
Tello, Don R., 82, 86, 87
Thames Estuary, 31
Thurlestone Inn, 147
Tilbury, 112-18
Tiverton, 40
Tobermory Bay, 147-9
Toby, 77
de Toledo, F., 98
Tomson, R., 91, 92
Topsham, 40
Trinidad Valencera, 123, 124, 134-36
Triumph 56, 57, 67, 78-80

Urcas, 19, 98, 123, 134, 146, 149
Ushant, 42

de Valdes, Diego Flores, 59, 60, 65, 95, 101,
    125, 152
de Valdes, Pedro, 49, 50, 58-60, 64, 132, 153
Vanegas, Capt. A., 101, 102
Vatican, 45
Venetian ambassador, 22, 151, 152
Victory, 57, 67
Vigo Bay, 26
Violet, 77

Walsingham, Sir F., 15, 16, 26-8, 33, 37, 39,
    41, 43, 71, 72, 95, 102, 103, 113, 126-29
Wells, 40
Weymouth, 40, 65, 131
White Bear, 56, 62, 79
Whitgift, Archbishop, 17
Williams, R., 114
Winchester, 17, 34
Wiveton, 40
Woodbridge, 40
Wynter, Sir W., 87, 96, 102

Yarmouth, 32

Zeeland Banks, 97, 100